D0455385

ILLINOIS

ART OF THE STATE

ART OF THE STATE

ILLINOIS

The Spirit of America

Text by Joanne Trestrail

Harry N. Abrams, Inc., Publishers

NEW YORK

This book was prepared for publication at
Walking Stick Press, San Francisco

Project staff:
Series Designer: Linda Herman
Series Editor: Diana Landau

For Harry N. Abrams, Inc.:
Series Editor: Ruth A. Peltason

Page 1: *Red-winged Blackbird* from *Heartland* by Wendell Minor, 1989. *Courtesy the artist*

Page 2: *Henry County Historical Quilt* by Dorothy Kirley, 1988. Each block on this quilt represents a township in Henry County, recording the county's landmarks and history. *Collection Marge Sommers. Courtesy Illinois Quilt Research Project, Early American Museum, Mahomet. Photo Will Zehr*

Library of Congress Cataloguing-in-Publication Data

Trestrail, Joanne.
Illinois / text by Joanne Trestrail.
p.   cm. — (Art of the state)
ISBN 0–8109–5567–9
1. Illinois Miscellanea.   2. Illinois Pictorial works.   I. Title.
II. Series.
F541.T74   1999
977.3—dc21   99–27135

Harry N. Abrams, Inc.
100 Fifth Avenue
New York, N.Y. 10011
www.abramsbooks.com

Abrams is a subsidiary of

LA MARTINIÈRE
GROUPE

Cover of a 1929 promotional calendar for John Deere & Company by R. A. Fox.
Deere & Company

"To the east were the moving waters as far as eye could follow. To the west a sea of grass as far as wind might reach."

Nelson Algren, Chicago: City on the Make, 1951

Look at any map of the United States and you see in a flash why Illinois exists: because it needs to. Somebody had to hold things together out in the vast, river-laced Midwest, and the job fell to Illinois. In the early years of westward settlement, the nation had a vital need for an inland outpost connected to the East Coast by navigable water—an accessible place close to the continent's center. A place like Chicago.

That Chicago ended up in Illinois and not in Wisconsin, as it might have, was due to the foresight of one Nathaniel Pope, a territorial delegate who guided the Illinois statehood bill through Congress in 1818. Pope arranged for the state's northern border to be pushed more than 50 miles north from its original location at the southern tip of Lake Michigan. In securing a Great Lakes shoreline for Illinois, he also secured its future; more than half the state's population today resides in the area Pope shrewdly annexed. He belongs to a long line of big thinkers Illinois can claim.

A topographical map of Illinois reveals another secret of its success. The state is almost surreally flat, leveled by advancing and retreating glaciers that ground down the land like giant, slow-moving slabs of sandpaper. The ice left behind rich sediments that would ease future cultivation. Forested areas lined the rivers; in between were treeless grasslands, developed over centuries, that further enriched the soil. The sheer denseness of the prairie would have posed serious problems for farmers but for the ingenuity of

The Art Class, Grand Detour by Oscar Daniel Soellner, c. 1935. *Illinois Historical Art Project*

another big thinker, John Deere, whose shiny steel plow sliced through the sod as the dull iron plows of New England never could.

Illinois weather can be harsh—bitter winters, sweltering summers, violent storms—so a certain hardiness is required of residents. This state is not known for producing or harboring flighty souls. It does, however, draw and keep those alert to the commercial possibilities of its lucky location and hospitable landscape, with space in all directions and no pesky mountains or coasts to limit growth. Illinois has always had a sense of being its own place—away from the East Coast yet aware of it—a sense that went public at the 1893 World's Columbian Exposition, which drew millions of visitors from near and far to Chicago. The influence of early business moguls—Marshall Field and Richard W. Sears in retail, George Pullman in railroads, Philip Armour and Gustavus F. Swift in meat-packing—is still felt. They were the power centers of the state's first century, but not even Illinoisans live by commerce alone. The activity it generates has produced a rich cultural life and citizens who are doers as well as thinkers—from architectural visionary Frank Lloyd Wright to artist-philosopher Laszlo Moholy-Nagy; from reporter-playwright Ben Hecht to talk-show queen Oprah Winfrey; and from blues progenitor Muddy Waters to baseball promoter Bill Veeck.

The split between Chicago and the rest of the state began early and endures. "Downstate" is generally understood to mean all of Illinois not encompassed by Chicago and its suburbs, whether or not technically "down." Scattered over this chunk of Midwest geography are midsized cities with

Clinton in Winter by Aaron Bohrod, c. 1930s, WPA mural for the Clinton post office. *Photo Mark G. Woods*
Opposite: Hotel Atlantic, Chicago. The city has welcomed tourists since its early years.

agricultural roots—Springfield (the capital), Rockford, Peoria, and Joliet being the largest. Its politics are strongly Republican. Illinois's southern regions were populated by settlers moving north across the Ohio River, and large areas remain southern in feel. Downstate's poet is Carl Sandburg; its iconic hero is honest, eloquent Abraham Lincoln—rail-splitter, emancipator, martyr.

Chicago's early residents, on the other hand, were mostly East Coasters and Europeans arriving by water after the Erie Canal's 1825 opening. Always a city of the world, raucous and rough, Chicago is at the same time highly sophisticated and occasionally even poetic. Its politics are strongly Democratic; its strength lies in absorbing the cultures and ideologies of far-flung places into its own unique synthesis. Illustrious Chicagoans have included the energetic empathist Jane Addams, architect Louis Sullivan, crime-buster Eliot Ness, and another tall, iconic hero, Michael Jordan—high-flying scorer, basketball artist, business tycoon.

Illinois remains both urban and rural at once. And flatness, it turns out, is good for much: operating farm equipment, riding bikes, walking far, erecting tall buildings, seeing a long way off. People stand out in a flat landscape, as does what they build. Native Americans, before they were driven from Illinois, constructed thousands of ceremonial and burial mounds, now so much a part of the landscape as to be one with it. These days Illinoisans build skyscrapers instead, but the principle is the same. They are leaving their mark. ❧

ILLINOIS

"Land of Lincoln"
21st State

Date of Statehood
DECEMBER 3, 1818

Capital
SPRINGFIELD

Bird
CARDINAL

Flower
VIOLET

Tree
WHITE OAK

Insect
MONARCH BUTTERFLY

Mineral
FLUORITE

Prairie grass
BIG BLUESTEM

The Illinois seal—portraying an American eagle perched on a prairie boulder, backed by a rising sun—is a respectful nod to the state's verdant past. The official flora and fauna likewise conjure up images of bygone times on the prairie—

Cardinal and violet awash with big bluestem, violets, and monarch butterflies—even if such landscapes are mostly a memory now. But the symbols are apt as well as pretty. When Illinois schoolchildren named the cardinal as the state bird in 1928 (trouncing the runner-up bluebird by 8,920 votes), they chose, consciously or not, a creature that shares some traits with the state's human residents. Happy near people or away from them, the cardinal lives in Illinois year-round—adaptable, flexible, cheerful (or is it stoic?) in the face of winter, one of the few species that sing in January. ❧

Fluorite

"State Sovereignty, National Union"

State motto

The Grass Is Always Bluer

Few states can claim an official prairie grass, but Illinois designated one in 1989. Big bluestem (*Andropogon gerardii*) was among the most widespread and abundant of the grasses that once covered the state. Green for much of the summer, the stem turns blue-purple as it matures. Its seed head, with three spiky projections, resembles a bird's foot, prompting the nickname "turkey foot." Big bluestem grows tall (3 to 10 feet) and dense, and its deep roots form very strong sod.

Above: **Big bluestem** (*Androgeon gerardii*). Photo Bill Glass/Root Resources. **Because big bluestem grows so densely, it often chokes out other grasses.** *Left: White Oak* by Anthony Tyznik, c. 1970–90. *The Morton Arboretum, Lisle* **Among the state's most abundant trees, white oaks can reach a height of 100 feet. The strong, beautiful wood is often harvested for cabinetry.** *Opposite below:* Fluorite (octahedral cleavage). Photo *Louise K. Broman/Root Resources*

Home-Grown Fossil

Despite its fearsome name, the Tully Monster (*Tullimonstrum gregarium*) is unlikely to star in a Hollywood blockbuster any time soon. Less than a foot long, with a long proboscis, this soft-bodied animal—probably a carnivore related to snails and other mollusks—swam in the ocean that covered much of Illinois about 300 million years ago. First found in 1958 by Francis Tully, who brought his specimen to Chicago's Field Museum of Natural History, Tully Monster fossils are unique to Illinois. They have been found in the Mazon Creek deposits in Will and Grundy counties and in open-pit coal mines.

The Nickname Game

"The Prairie State" is Illinois's unofficial slogan, though true, uncultivated grasslands are now rare. The word lingers in place names (Prairie Grove, Prairie View); as an urban synonym for "vacant lot"; and, most elegantly, in Frank Lloyd Wright's strongly horizontal Prairie architecture.

Chicago's nickname, "The Windy City," refers not to wind but to self-aggrandizement. The tag was coined in 1890 by a newspaper editor as a put-down to Chicago's puffery as prospective host of the World's Columbian Exposition. The city's other faint-praising moniker, "Second City," was laid on it by A. J. Liebling in *The New Yorker*. Population-wise, Chicago *was* the nation's second city for many years, but Los Angeles passed it in the 1980s.

Left: Lincoln Logs, c. 1955; the patriotic toy was invented by John Lloyd Wright, son of Frank. *Chicago Historical Society. Above:* Interior of the state capitol. *Photo Tim Bieber/Image Bank*

Of Thee We Sing

Like most of Illinois's official emblems, the state song barely recognizes the great metropolis of Chicago. But the "toddlin' town" makes its own music.

"Illinois"

By the rivers gently flowing, Illinois, Illinois,
O'er thy prairies verdant growing, Illinois, Illinois,
Comes an echo on the breeze.
Rustling thro' the leafy trees, and its mellow tones
    are these,
Illinois, Illinois,
And its mellow tones are these, Illinois.

Words by C. H. Chamberlain, music by Archibald Johnston

"Chicago"

Chicago, Chicago, that toddlin' town—
Chicago, Chicago, I'll show you around—
Bet your bottom dollar you'll lose the blues
    in Chicago, Chicago—
The town that Billy Sunday could not shut down.

Words and music by Fred Fisher

Chicago Dawgs

Even more than deep-dish pizza, a Chicago hot dog is the city's native food. Its tightly prescribed preparation: take a slender, Vienna Beef–brand skinless frank, steam to a medium crunch (never boil, grill, or fry), and serve on a warm steamed bun (which may have poppy seeds for added flavor) with these mandatory condiments and garnishes:

Yellow mustard
Freshly chopped onion
Sweet relish (the
    bright-green kind)
Two wedges of tomato
New-pickle spear
1–2 hot sport peppers
    (peperoncini)
Dash of celery salt

The most authentic versions (other than your own) can be consumed at Byron's, Superdawg, Gold Coast Dogs, and Fluky's.

Adapted from a feature by Jonathan Gold in Travel & Leisure, *March 1999*

Left: Chicago Theater marquee, a Loop landmark. *Photo Andrea Pistolesi/Image Bank. Right:* Larger-than-life wieners draw crowds to Superdawg on Milwaukee Avenue, Chicago. *Photo Susan Anderson*

c. 1000 B.C.–A.D. 1500   Mound-building people inhabit the region.

1673   Louis Jolliet and Father Jacques Marquette discover the Illinois country.

1680   Robert Cavalier, Sieur de la Salle, reaches Illinois, erects Fort Crevecoeur ("heartbreak") at Peoria.

1717   Illinois country placed under government of Louisiana.

1783   Treaty of Paris extends United States boundary to Mississippi.

1787   Northwest Territory organized.

1800   Indiana Territory, which includes Illinois, is formed.

1803   Louisiana Purchase puts Illinois in center of U.S.; Fort Dearborn founded.

1809   Illinois becomes a territory.

1812   Fort Dearborn massacre.

1818   Illinois becomes 21st state.

1832   The Black Hawk War, last episode of Indian warfare in Illinois.

1833   Town of Chicago incorporated. Indians cede last Illinois land.

1837   John Deere invents steel plow.

1842   First train on Northern Cross railroad, Meredosia to Springfield.

1846   Mormons leave Nauvoo, two years after mob kills Joseph and Hyrum Smith.

1847   The Midwest's first Jewish congregation founded in Chicago.

1848   Illinois and Michigan canal opened.

1856   Illinois Central railroad completed.

1858   Lincoln–Douglas debates.

1860   Lincoln nominated for president by the new Republican Party.

1865   Union Stock Yards open in Chicago.

1867   Illinois Industrial University established at Urbana.

1870   Chicago White Stockings baseball team (became Cubs, not White Sox) plays first inter-city game, defeating New Orleans.

1871   George Pullman opens shop to build "palace cars." The Chicago Fire.

1886   Labor meeting in Haymarket ends in violence; at least 11 people are killed.

1889   Jane Addams and Ellen Gates Starr found Hull House. Louis Sullivan's Auditorium Theatre is dedicated.

1891   Women granted suffrage in school elections; Theodore Thomas organizes Chicago Symphony Orchestra; Monadnock Building opens.

1892 Newberry Library and Art Institute open. First elevated rapid transit line opens for service in Chicago.

1893 World's Columbian Exposition; retail magnate Marshall Field endows museum of natural history.

1894 Pullman strike is broken by U.S. troops.

1900 Flow of Chicago River is reversed.

1906 Upton Sinclair's exposé of meat-packing industry, *The Jungle*, is published.

1909 Daniel Burnham and Edward Bennett's *Plan of Chicago* is published.

1912 Harriet Monroe starts *Poetry: A Magazine of Verse*.

1914 Weeghman Park (now Wrigley Field) opens.

1918 Goodman School of Drama opens.

1919 In "Black Sox" scandal, White Sox players throw the World Series.

1920 Prohibition (18th amendment) takes effect on Al Capone's 21st birthday.

1924 Nathan Leopold and Richard Loeb are convicted of murdering a 14-year old but spared the death penalty.

1925 Tribune Tower opens.

1929 Seven men are killed by Capone

THE TRIBUNE TOWER.

henchmen in St. Valentine's Day Massacre. Civic Opera House opens in Chicago.

1933–34 Century of Progress fair.

1938 Mies van der Rohe arrives at Armour Institute (Illinois Institute of Technology).

1942 Scientists led by Enrico Fermi at the University of Chicago achieve world's first self-sustaining nuclear reaction.

1953 Hugh Hefner's *Playboy* magazine first published.

1955 Richard J. Daley elected mayor of Chicago.

1959 St. Lawrence Seaway is completed, giving state a direct outlet to Atlantic.

1967 Picasso sculpture unveiled in Chicago's Loop.

1968 Protesters clash with police during Democratic National Convention.

1973 The 110-story Sears Tower, then the tallest building in the world, is topped out.

1979 Jane Byrne, first female mayor of Chicago, is elected.

1983 Harold Washington, first African-American mayor of Chicago, is elected.

1993 Devastating floods cover 500,000 acres of land in Illinois, causing $1.5 billion in damage.

Even the least observant bird flying over Illinois would be struck by the state's flatness, the legacy of glaciers that leveled nearly 90 percent of the land. The last ice sheet melted about 25,000 years ago, leaving behind a thick layer of till—mineral-rich particles from other places. Moraines of piled-up till rise above the general flatness; Indian mounds also stand out. The state's highest point, Charles Mound, is only 1,241 feet above sea level.

That's not to say the landscape lacks appeal. Unbroken vistas of field and sky greet a traveler driving through

the state's central sections. Gentle hills and woodlands line the waterways that lace inland Illinois and mark its borders. Far south, in the area known as Egypt, the Ozark Plateaus define a rougher terrain. And be-

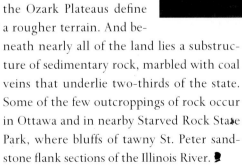

neath nearly all of the land lies a substructure of sedimentary rock, marbled with coal veins that underlie two-thirds of the state. Some of the few outcroppings of rock occur in Ottawa and in nearby Starved Rock State Park, where bluffs of tawny St. Peter sandstone flank sections of the Illinois River. ❧

Above: Landscape in Early Fall by James D. Butler, 1988. *Courtesy the artist*
Opposite: Matthiessen State Park. Wooded areas along Illinois's waterways provide contrast to unbroken vistas of field and sky. *Photo Jason Lindsey*

Climate and Cataclysm

Illinois knows nothing of volcanoes or hurricanes. Earthquakes, though technically possible, are not an imminent threat. Untamed nature manifests here mostly in the form of extreme heat and cold, violent thundershowers and snowstorms, and occasional devastating floods like those that crippled much of the Midwest in 1993. Highly destructive tornadoes may occur at any time of year.

Prairie at Chain O'Lakes State Park. Relatively little authentic prairie remains in Illinois, where cultivated fields of corn and soybeans (and urban development) have replaced it. The few surviving patches of grassland are carefully protected.
Photo Jason Lindsey

Grassland to Farmland

The first white settlers to view the prairie were amazed by the vast, treeless sweeps of land stretching toward the horizon, a sea of tall, densely growing grass. The Native Americans who preceded them had planted crops near rivers, hacking small plots out of forests rather than fight the tough sod, and few explorers ventured beyond those woodlands. An early visitor, Captain Basil Hall, remarked on the prairie's beauty in the 1820s: "In the early stages of its growth the grass is interspersed with little flowers, the violet, the strawberry blossom, and others of the most delicate structure. When the grass grows higher these disappear, and taller flowers displaying more lively colors take their place."

Below the grasslands, undisturbed for millennia, lies an unrocky soil whose fertility drew farmers from distant southern and eastern states. When the self-scouring steel plow made their cultivation viable, the prairies began to disappear, an acre at a time.

"ILLINOIS...BEARS THE CHARACTER OF A COUNTRY WHICH HAS been inhabited by a nation skilled like the English in all the ornamental arts of life, especially in landscape gardening.... [T]he velvet lawns, the flower gardens, the stately parks, scattered at graceful intervals by the decorous hand of art...all suggest more of the masterly mind of man than the prodigal, but careless, motherly love of nature."

Margaret Fuller, "The Fox River Valley and the Rock River Country," 1843

Above: **Greater prairie chicken (*Tympanuchus cupido*). A member of the pheasant family, this wildfowl once was found throughout the central U.S. and Canada. Its numbers diminished as the prairies were replaced by cultivated fields and grazing lands.** *Photo Richard Day/Midwestock Left: Summer Evening by* **Frank Charles Peyraud, 1927. The Swiss-born Peyraud's most popular work may have been a cyclorama of the Chicago Fire.** *Illinois Historical Art Project*

A Wealth of Waterways

Illinois's borders are largely defined by rivers—the Mississippi to the west, the Ohio to the south, and the Wabash to the southeast. Within the state, the Illinois and the Rock Rivers are the largest; both flow into the Mississippi. While all the state's rivers see heavy recreational use, the Illinois Waterway—composed of the Chicago, Illinois, and Des Plaines Rivers, along with the Chicago Sanitary and Ship Canal—is also a busy commercial artery, facilitating transport of coal, grain, and other bulk cargoes between Chicago and the Mississippi.

The land on which Chicago stands was once the bottom of an ancient lake, which over time pooled its resources and became Lake Michigan. It's the second most voluminous of the Great Lakes, which together hold about 20 percent of the world's fresh surface water. In a landlocked state, Lake Michigan is a rare source of natural beauty on a grand scale, as well as Chicago's source of drinking water. Wildly, dramatically dangerous one day, serene the next, the lake has many moods, none predictable.

"WE WENT DRIFTING DOWN INTO A BIG BEND, AND THE night clouded up and got hot. The river was very wide, and was walled with solid timber on both sides; you couldn't see a break in it hardly ever, or a light. We talked about Cairo, and wondered whether we would know it when we got to it."

Mark Twain, The Adventures of Huckleberry Finn, *1884*

The Mississippi River near Delabar State Park. *Photo Robert Shaw, Wild Perceptions. Opposite above: Goose Island, Chicago by Albert François Fleury, 1898. Illinois Historical Art Project. Opposite below:* **The middle fork of the Vermilion River, a designated National Wild and Scenic River, in Kickapoo State Park.** *Photo Robert Shaw, Wild Perceptions*

Right: Artist's rendering of thunderbird petroglyph by Mississippian natives, c. A.D. 900–1500, at Millstone Bluff Archaeological site in Shawnee National Forest. *Wild Perceptions. Below:* Frog pipe, Mississippian, c. A.D. 1100. *Illinois State Museum. Photo Gary Andrashko. Opposite above:* Portrait of Black Hawk by Homer Henderson, c. 1870, after a portrait by Charles Bird King, 1837. *Chicago Historical Society. Opposite below:* Hopewell bowl, Middle Woodland culture, c. A.D. 150. *Center for American Archaeology Photo Kenneth B. Farnsworth*

The First Illinoisans

Ceremonial and burial mounds provide tantalizing glimpses of Illinois's earliest inhabitants. These immense earth-and-rubble constructions include the largest earthwork in the world, Cahokia or Monks Mound, near East St. Louis. Built by people of the Middle Mississippian culture, who lived here about A.D. 900, it's surrounded by 84 other mounds. Northwestern Illinois is home to several effigy mounds in the shapes of animals: there is a serpent-shaped mound near Galena, and a bird with outstretched wings near where Smallpox Creek joins the Mississippi.

When French explorers reached the region in the 17th century, the native people they encountered were the Illinois, or Illiniwek (spellings vary), an Algonquian-speaking confederation. The Illinois lived along waterways in multifamily rectangular houses, planted corn, and periodically burned off prairie grasses to expose game. They worshiped Manitou, the Great Spirit; looked forward to an afterlife; and buried their dead in fine clothing along

Native Names

Chicago Thirty-nine spellings (*chicagou, checagou, cikakunge* among them) have been found for this word meaning wild garlic, leek, onion, or "stinking weed," which grew in the area at the time of its first settlement.

Illinois A French derivation from *iniwek* or *iniok,* meaning men; the collective name of a confederacy of tribes that occupied the region.

Peoria Probably from Illinois-Miami *Pireouah,* meaning "turkey."

Skokie Likely derived from *Kitchiwap chkoku,* a Potawatomi term for a great marsh.

Wabash Possibly a corruption of Miami *Wahbah* (white) *shikki* (pure, inanimate, and natural).

with jewelry and other small items. Disease and intertribal warfare with the Iroquois, Fox, and Sioux decimated the Illinois population over the decades. By 1832, when the last land cession treaty was signed and they were driven from the state, they numbered fewer than 100. ❧

Above: Defense, bas-relief by Henry Hering, Michigan Avenue Bridge pylon, 1920. *Photo Scott Barrow. Right:* Portrait of Jean Baptiste Point du Sable by Charles Dawson. *Chicago Historical Society*

The first Europeans to lay eyes on Illinois were fur trader Louis Jolliet and Catholic missionary Jacques Marquette, in 1673. French missions soon attracted more colonists; most farmed along the Mississippi. Between 1689 and 1763, the French, the British, and the powerful Iroquois Confederacy fought for domination of the continent. In 1774, England's Parliament declared the land that's now Illinois to be part of Quebec, one of several acts that precipitated the American Revolution. When the war ended, the victorious colonists handed over their claims to the area north of the Ohio River to the federal government.

The earliest non-natives in Chicago settled around Fort Dearborn, which the United States had built in 1803. (The town's first permanent resident—a Haitian trader named Jean Baptiste Point du Sable—had taken up residence some time before 1790.) When the War of 1812 broke out, the Indians left in the Illinois

Territory—mostly Potawatomi, Kickapoo, Sac, and Fox—sided with the British against the Americans, with whom they had exchanged land for money and gifts. Early in the war, the 67-person garrison at Fort Dearborn, along with other settlers bound for the safer haven of Detroit, were attacked by supposedly friendly Indians; two-thirds of the Americans were killed in what became known as the Fort Dearborn Massacre. 🔫

Indian Treaty of Greenville. Artist unknown, 1795. Following their defeat at the Battle of Fallen Timbers in northwestern Ohio in 1794, Native Americans relinquished much land, opening parts of the Northwest Territory to white settlement. *Chicago Historical Society*

Galena Harbor, 1852 by Bayard Taylor, 1852. The town of Galena was laid out in 1826 and flourished until about 1860, when lead mining declined in the region. *Michael McCoy Collection Opposite above: Sun capstone from the Mormon Temple at Nauvoo. Photo Terry Farmer. Opposite below: General Grant by Frank Pierson Richards, c. 1880–88. Grant was a Galena resident. Illinois State Museum*

Growing the State

When Illinois became a state in 1818, Chicago was a bare-bones outpost of traders; most of the population lived elsewhere. Strained relationships with Native Americans continued beyond the end of the War of 1812, and in 1832, the Black Hawk War broke out, with the Sac making one last effort to reclaim their lands. After several bloody battles, Black Hawk, leader of the Sac and Fox, surrendered; the next year the Potawatomi and two other remaining tribes gave up all claims to territory in northeastern Illinois.

With the threat of warfare quieted, new settlers arrived in ever greater numbers, moving inland as they learned to cultivate the tough prairie sod. The momentous opening of the Erie Canal in 1825 brought emigrants flooding in from the Northeast; Chicago's population jumped from about 200 in 1832 to 1,400 in 1833. Completion of the Illinois and Michigan Canal and the railroads' arrival in the early 1850s further spurred the growth of both city and state.

The Mormon Exodus

Nauvoo, a Mississippi River town established by Mormons, was Illinois's largest settlement in the 1840s. When Mormon leader Joseph Smith declared himself a candidate for U.S. president in 1844, hostilities simmered. Dissenting Mormons started a newspaper attacking polygamy; Smith had the press destroyed. While jailed for that offense, he and his brother Hyrum were killed by a mob. Two years later, Mormons led by Brigham Young left Nauvoo for good on the long trail to Utah.

Come leave the fields of childhood
Worn out by long employ
And travel west and settle
In the State of Illinois.

Anonymous, "Westward the Star of Empire Moves," in the Boston Post, *1849*

"The prairie-lawyer, master of us all."

Vachel Lindsay, "Abraham Lincoln Walks at Midnight," 1914

Abraham Lincoln, born in Kentucky in 1809, came to Illinois when his family moved to a farm west of Decatur in 1830. Almost entirely unschooled, he taught himself mathematics and law, read Shakespeare and the poetry of Robert Burns, participated in a debating society. The only U.S. president to hold a patent, he invented a flotation system to buoy vessels over shoals. And he was a diligent, successful lawyer, covering 14 counties of Illinois's 8th Judicial Circuit from 1849 to 1860.

Lincoln's antislavery stance was well known even before his famous 1858 debates with Stephen Douglas. As president in 1863, with the country mired in the Civil War, he issued the Emancipation Proclamation, a step toward the dismantling of slavery. He did not live to see its official end. Shot by John Wilkes Booth on April 14, 1865, he died the next day, eight months before the Thirteenth Amendment was finally ratified. His death set off shock waves around the world, but particularly in Illinois. A special funeral train slowly crossed the country before reaching its destination at Oak Ridge Cemetery, near his home in Springfield. ❧

"A. NOW THINKS THAT THE AGGREGATE OF ALL HIS schooling did not amount to one year. He was never in a college or Academy as a student; and never inside of a college or academy building till since he had a law-license. What he has in the way of education, he has picked up."

Lincoln on Lincoln: from an autobiographical sketch, 1860, written after being nominated as candidate for president

When lilacs last in the dooryard bloomed,
And the great star early drooped in the western
    sky in the night,
I mourned, and yet shall mourn with
    ever-returning spring.

Walt Whitman, "When Lilacs Last in the Dooryard Bloomed," 1865. Along with "O Captain, My Captain!" this is one of two Whitman poems memorializing Lincoln.

Lincoln Locales

Tourists flock to sites important in the life of Abraham Lincoln. They include:

New Salem   Reconstructed log buildings mark the settlement where Lincoln worked as a store clerk and postmaster.

Lincoln Home   Meticulous restoration of the only home Lincoln ever owned.

Old State Capitol   In a speech here Lincoln declared that "A house divided against itself will not stand."

Lincoln Tomb   The 16th president is laid to rest in Oak Ridge Cemetery.

Lincoln–Douglas Debate sites   Alton, Charleston, Freeport, Galesburg, Jonesboro, Ottawa, Quincy

Left: Lincoln–Douglas Debate at Charleston, September 18, 1858 by Robert Marshall Root, c. 1918. State Historical Library of Illinois. Opposite above: Lincoln with son Tad, February 9, 1864. Photo Anthony Berger. Opposite below: The Railsplitter. Artist unknown, c. 1858. Both, Chicago Historical Society

N.C. THOMPSON'S REAPER WORKS.

The Plow That Tamed the Plains

When Vermont emigré John Deere opened his blacksmith's shop in Grand Detour, Illinois, in 1836, he made an alarming discovery: the cast-iron plows that worked so well in New England's sandy soil were unmanageable in the heavier, stickier soil of the Midwest. Deere's shiny, self-scouring steel plow, which did not have to be laboriously cleaned off every few steps, was a breakthrough for farmers. (He got the idea, it's said, by watching his mother's shiny needle slide

JOHN DEERE
MOLINE, ILL.

through rough fabric.) By 1848 Deere's factory in Moline was producing 1,000 plows a year. The company would go on to manufacture a wide range of farm implements, including cultivators, planters, and tractors.

Illinois continued to grow innovations along with bumper crops of corn and soybeans. Cyrus McCormick, the Virginia-born inventor of the first successful reaping machine, turned his small manufacturing operation into a giant one when he moved to Chicago in 1847. McCormick's modern business methods included the then-new ideas of deferred payment plans, guarantees, and testimonials in advertising. His company eventually became International Harvester (now Navistar).

A Better Barbed Wire

Although he didn't invent barbed wire, Joseph Glidden of DeKalb improved on a two-stranded version he'd seen at a county fair in 1873 and successfully patented his design. Produced in quantity, the fencing material was a simple, relatively cheap solution to the problem of separating livestock from crops.

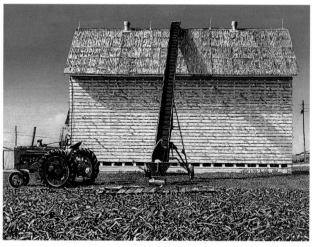

Illinois Farmscape #18 by Harold Gregor, 1976. Collection George M. Irwin. Photo Ken Kashian/ Lakeview Museum of Arts and Sciences. Opposite above: *N. C. Thompson's Reaper Works,* attributed to George J. Robertson, c. 1850. *Illinois State Museum.* Opposite below: Since 1876, a leaping deer has been part of all Deere & Company trademarks. *Deere & Company*

Driving Hogs to the Chicago Market, **engraving from** *Harper's Weekly,* **1868. Thousands of hogs, sheep, and cattle were shipped by rail every day to be slaughtered at the Union Stock Yards. Cooked meats packed at the Yards were one of many foodstuffs prepared for Union troops in the city during the Civil War.** *Chicago Historical Society*

"Hog Butcher to the World"

Chicago's meat-packing industry was already the largest in the world when the vast Union Stock Yards opened on Christmas Day, 1865. The enterprise dominated the city's Southwest Side, with hundreds of acres of stock pens stretching in all directions. Over the decades, the Stock Yards employed thousands of Irish, German, Polish, Hungarian, Czech, Yugoslavian, African-American, and Lithuanian immigrants. During World War I, 15 million animals a year were butchered in Chicago, producing almost 9 million pounds of meat a day. Fortunes were built by Gustavus F. Swift, Philip Armour, and other packing tycoons who, it was said, used every part of a hog but its squeal.

Upton Sinclair's 1906 novel *The Jungle* shocked readers with its description of dire conditions for workers at the yards, and led to higher standards for the then carelessly regulated industry. Dirty and dangerous, perilous to health even at the best of times, the Stock Yards announced their presence to the rest of the city by their unmistakable odor. Not until the yards closed for good in 1971 did the smell disappear, but their impact on Chicago is likely to linger indefinitely.

"THERE WAS NO HEAT UPON THE KILLING BEDS; THE MEN MIGHT exactly as well have worked out of doors all winter. For that matter, there was very little heat anywhere in the building, except in the cooking rooms and such places.... On the killing beds you were apt to be covered with blood, and it would freeze solid; if you leaned against a pillar, you would freeze to that, and if you put your hand upon the blade of your knife, you would run a chance of leaving your skin on it."

Upton Sinclair, The Jungle, *1906*

Advertising ephemera for a Chicago meat packer. The introduction of the refrigerated rail car in the 1870s made it possible to ship meat all over the country. The Stock Yards were linked to every major rail line coming into Chicago. *Private collection*

"THE BEST IN THE MARKET."

Railroad Fever

Around 1850, America entered an era of intensive railroad building, with cities scrambling for position on the most important lines. Chicago's location made it a hub for both north–south and east–west routes, with the 320-mile barrier of Lake Michigan forcing railroads to aim for its southern end. The construction of just one line—the Illinois Central, running the length of the state and beyond—was an engineering marvel, a bigger public works project than the Erie Canal. Completed in 1856, at 705.5 miles it was the world's longest rail line. Railroad companies platted and built towns along their rights-of-way, and towns passed by sometimes relocated themselves to be on the new lines.

By 1860 Chicago was the nation's rail center, with 11 trunk lines connecting it to other cities and states. Access to raw materials and customers for its goods hastened the city's commercial growth. Rails for the Illinois tracks

The Pullman Palace Car

One-time cabinetmaker George Pullman pioneered the sleeper car for long-distance travel, and in 1880 built a model town to house his Pullman Palace Car workers far from the evil influences of the city. The violent Pullman Strike of 1894 came in reaction to the company's high-handed policies, and it introduced two important social reformers: attorney Clarence Darrow, who defended strike leader Eugene V. Debs, and Hull House founder Jane Addams, who led an investigation of the strike.

Left: A Chicago & Eastern Illinois Railroad train, c. 1944. Photographer unknown (Chicago Photo Club). *Chicago Historical Society. Below:* The Wabash Avenue El, 1983. *Photo John Lewis Stage/Image Bank*

once had to make a long trip from England by way of New Orleans or the Great Lakes, but in 1865, the first steel rails made in the U.S. came from the Chicago Rolling Mills. Even today, Illinois handles more railroad cars than any other state.

> All along the southbound odyssey
> The train pulls out of Kankakee
> And rolls along past houses, farms,
>   and fields....
>
> *Lyrics from "The City of New Orleans"*
> *by Steve Goodman*

THE MISSION TYPE

The ALHAMBRA — No. 2090 "Already Cut" and Fitted — Honor Bilt — $1,969.00

SEARS ROEBUCK AND CO. CHICAGO

Assembly required:
Plans and materials for
building do-it-yourself
houses were popular
with Sears customers.
*Sears, Roebuck and Co.
Archives*

Two giant catalog retailers grew up side by side in Chicago, serving essentially the same customers. Aaron Montgomery Ward founded Montgomery Ward & Company, the nation's oldest mail-order business, in 1872. As a traveling dry-goods salesman, he'd had the idea of buying merchandise in bulk from manufacturers and selling it to farmers by mail. The first mail-order listing put out by watch dealers Richard W. Sears and Alvah Roebuck offered only watches and jewelry, but by 1893 their catalog included clothing, furniture, and other household items. The company soon became known as the place to buy everything, from plans and building materials for a house to a teapot to put in the kitchen cupboard—also from Sears, of course. ❧

"Give the lady what she wants."

Marshall Field

Mr. Field's Store

For well over a century, the department-store customer in Chicago has counted on Marshall Field's reassuring presence on State Street. Its holiday windows, Walnut Room restaurant, Frango mints, and outdoor clocks are part of the city's collective memory. When Marshall Field bought out partner Levi Z. Leiter in 1881, customer service was a relatively new concept. Field allowed merchandise returns, highly unusual at the time. And when he heard a manager argue with a customer, he intervened, saying, "Give the lady what she wants"—a phrase that became the store's unofficial motto.

"[THIS] CELEBRATED WESTERN MERCHANT… is an example to be studied with profit by every farm boy, by every office boy, by every clerk and artisan—yes, and by every middle-aged business man."

Theodore Dreiser, c. 1900

Marshall Field and Company catalog cover, *Fashions of the Hour,* January 1920. The Field name endures on department stores (now owned by Dayton Hudson) and also on the Field Museum of Natural History. *Marshall Field's Photo Archive. Left:* Ad for Doublemint gum, 1960. In Chicago, the name Wrigley means not only chewing gum but also the Cubs' ballpark, Wrigley Field, and the landmark Wrigley Building on North Michigan Avenue. *Courtesy Wm. Wrigley, Jr. Company*

Chicago has been called a living museum of architecture, with many of its commercial structures designed by the leading architects of the last 150 years. The city was home to William Le Baron Jenney's 10-story Home Insurance Building (demolished in 1931), considered the first skyscraper. As early problems with foundation engineering, frame construction, fireproofing, and elevator safety were solved, it soon became clear that when it came to building high, only the sky would be the limit. In its day, Burnham & Root's Monadnock Building (1889–91) was the world's tallest office building at 16 stories. The much loftier Sears Tower by Skidmore, Owings & Merrill (1968–74) soars 110 stories, tallest in the world until 1996. Other standout buildings include Mies van der Rohe's glassy, abstract Chicago Federal Center (1959–74) and SOM's cross-hatched Hancock Center. ✏

Form Follows Function

Louis Sullivan, widely considered the spiritual father of modern U.S. architecture, was a prominent figure in the Chicago School, which included other practitioners of early skyscraper design. In 1881 he formed a partnership with Dankmar Adler, and the two produced more than 100 buildings. Sullivan's designs combined bold architectural forms with graceful ornamentation, often evoking themes from nature. His axiom "Form follows function" expressed his belief that a building's purpose should serve as the starting point for its design.

Above: Bold structural cross-bracing makes the 100-story Hancock Center (Skidmore, Owings & Merrill, 1969) a landmark on the downtown skyline. *Chicago Historical Society. Photo Hedrich-Blessing Left:* The Auditorium Theatre (1887–89) showcases Louis Sullivan's genius for ornamentation. *Photo Judith Bromley Opposite: Carson Pirie Scott Store* by Albert Fleury, 1903. *Chicago Historical Society*

The Rush for Life Over the Randolph Street Bridge, sketch by John R. Chapin, 1871, from Harper's Weekly. Chicago Historical Society

Out of the Ashes

Nearly three square miles of central Chicago, including the entire commercial district, were destroyed in the Great Fire of 1871. The blaze started in a barn belonging to Patrick and Catherine O'Leary at 137 DeKoven Street, southwest of downtown, at about 9 p.m. on Sunday, October 8, and burned for 36 hours. Although it almost certainly was *not* ignited by the O'Learys' cow kicking over a lantern, that colorful myth persisted for generations.

High winds, dry conditions, and large amounts of flammable building material in the city—including wooden roofs, raised sidewalks, and streets paved with pine blocks—contributed to the devastation. At least 300 people died and 90,000 residents, about a third of the city's population, were left homeless. The limestone water tower and its adjacent pumping station were among the few buildings in the fire's path that survived. These two "castellated Gothic" structures, which once stood alone amid the charred ruins, are now dwarfed by the towering malls, hotels, and office buildings of the city's most glamorous shopping district, North Michigan Avenue.

Men said at vespers: "All is well!"
In one wild night the city fell;
Fell shrines of prayer and marts of grain
Before the fiery hurricane.

On threescore spires had sunset shone,
Where ghastly sunrise looked on none.
Men clasped each other's hands, and said:
"The City of the West is dead!"

John Greenleaf Whittier, from "Chicago," c. 1871

Above: Mrs. Catherine O'Leary Milking Daisy by Norman Rockwell, c. 1935. Today, firefighters train at the Chicago Fire Academy, built on the site of the O'Leary barn on the city's Near Southwest Side. Chicago Historical Society

Foreign Aid

When word of the fire's devastation got out, British writers expressed their sympathy by organizing a book drive. The English Book Donation drew more than 8,000 volumes from Queen Victoria, Benjamin Disraeli, John Stuart Mill, Dante Gabriel Rossetti, and others and led to the establishment of a free public library in Chicago.

Proposed plaza on Michigan Avenue west of the Field Museum, watercolor attributed to Chris U. Bagge, 1907–8. In the illustrations for the *Plan of Chicago*, horse-drawn vehicles and automobiles peacefully coexist on broad, tree-lined boulevards, while pedestrians stroll nearby. *Chicago Historical Society*

Blueprint for Urban Living

Overnight, the Great Fire catapulted Chicago into the modern age. The city began to rebuild before the ashes had cooled; nonmasonry construction was banned within the city limits. Architects embraced the project of creating a new commercial center, transforming former residential sections into business and cultural districts. As the population boomed, urban planning fell by the wayside, the victim of eager opportunism.

Order began to emerge from the chaos with the 1909 publication of architect Daniel Burnham's *Plan of Chicago*. His blueprint for intracity transportation called for the widening of arterial streets and a double-decked boulevard in the central area along the Chicago River. At the same time, the City

Council instituted an orderly address-numbering system that used the intersection of State and Madison as a 0/0 center point. But perhaps the most resonant aspect of Burnham's plan was his vision for grand public spaces—especially parks—around the city, and forest preserves on its outskirts. His dream of a lakefront free of private ownership endures today in the form of a nearly city-long swath of landscaped public space, one of Chicago's great aesthetic treasures.

"MAKE NO LITTLE PLANS; THEY HAVE NO MAGIC TO STIR MEN'S blood and probably themselves will not be realized. Make big plans; aim high in hope and work, remembering that a noble, logical diagram once recorded will never die, but long after we are gone will be a living thing, asserting itself with ever-growing insistency.... Let your watchword be order and your beacon beauty."

Daniel Burnham, 1907

Above: **Buckingham Fountain. The pink marble fountain, illuminated at night, is an important focal point in Grant Park, one of Daniel Burnham's grand public spaces.** *Photo Scott Barrow. Left:* **Aerial view of Lincoln Park, looking south. Burnham's Plan led to the creation of landscaped parks along the lakefront and in outlying neighborhoods.** *Photo Mark Segal/Tony Stone Images*

Food Firsts at the Fair

Americans got their first taste of these treats at the 1893 Exposition:

Cracker Jack
Aunt Jemima syrup
Cream of Wheat
Shredded Wheat
Pabst beer
Juicy Fruit gum
Hamburgers

Chicago's prominence as a site for trade shows and political conventions stems from a long tradition. The 1893 World's Columbian Exposition—which ostensibly celebrated the 400th anniversary of Columbus's arrival in the Americas, but also announced to the world that Chicago was up and running after the fire—was the first large-scale spectacle the city hosted. Spread along the south lakefront, the nearly 700-acre Exposition had Daniel Burnham as chief planner and Frederick Law Olmsted in charge of landscaping.

The fair's eye-popping White City was a classical stage set in molded plaster; the halls' pillared, porticoed facades had little functional connection to their cavernous interiors. (Modernists, Louis Sullivan among them, were contemptuous of the fair's retro-Euro look.) Nighttime illumination of the White City gave most spectators their first look at electricity, introduced four years earlier at the Paris Exposition. Some 27 million visitors were also dazzled by the world's first Ferris wheel, a gargantuan steel structure whose 36 cars each held 60 people. The fair's only permanent building, the Palace of Fine Arts, later became the Museum of Science and Industry. ∎

Above: Ferris wheel poster, c. 1893. *Chicago Historical Society. Left:* Havoline Thermometer at the Century of Progress International Exposition, Chicago, 1933. This more subdued fair managed to turn a profit even in mid-Depression. *Private collection. Opposite: World's Columbian Exposition, Chicago, 1893 by John Ross Key, c. 1890s. Christie's Images*

HAVOLINE THERMOMETER *Century of Progress International Exposition* CHICAGO 1933

"SURELY THE BRIGHT, CHEERFUL buildings of the Fair must have a gladdening effect upon the future of building in the rapidly developing West."

New York journalist Gustav Kobbé, "Sights at the Fair" in The Century Magazine, *1893*

Illinois has long been a showcase for public art. Its parks are filled with monuments to the nation's heroes; murals adorn many post offices and outdoor spaces. Statues of Lincoln abound, the most distinguished being Lorado Taft's portrayal of the young lawyer in Urbana. In Chicago, the 1967 unveiling of the untitled steel sculpture natives call "the Picasso" whetted citizens' appetite for public art; the city today is home to an unusual number of works by internationally important artists on year-round display. They include Alexander Calder's *Flamingo* (1974), a steel stabile at Federal Center plaza; *Chicago* by Joan Miro, a concrete, bronze, and ceramic tile piece at 69 W. Washington; and *Dawn Shadows* by Louise Nevelson (1983) at 200 W. Madison, whose form and materials were inspired by the nearby elevated train. Outside Chicago, a notable contemporary work is Michael Heizer's earthwork *Effigy Tumuli,* in LaSalle County. Out of strip-mining spoil, Heizer created giant animal sculptures inspired by Illinois's Native American effigy mounds (see page 87). ❧

Lorado Taft

Native-born sculptor Lorado Taft (1860–1936) was a major figure on Illinois's art scene in the early 20th century, his heroic, brooding figures inviting comparison with Rodin's. Many successful artists trained in his classes at Chicago's Art Institute. His public monuments around the state include *Fountain of Time,* his masterpiece in Chicago's Washington Park; the *World War I Victory Monument* in Danville; the *Black Hawk* monument on the Rock River near Oregon (where Taft and other artists in 1898 founded Eagle's Nest Art Colony, which thrived in the 1920s); *Pioneers of the Prairies,* Taft's memorial to his parents in his birthplace, Elmwood; and in White Hall, the *Memorial to Annie Louise Keller,* a teacher who lost her life saving pupils from a tornado in 1927.

"Yippie" leader Abbie Hoffman prepares for battle during the 1968 Democratic Convention in Chicago. *Opposite above: Portrait of Jane Addams by Alice Kellogg Tyler, 1893. Both, Chicago Historical Society. Opposite below: Michigan Boulevard with Mayor Daley by Red Grooms, 1969.* Painted the year after Daley quashed convention protests, this work depicts his outsized impact on Chicago. *The Metropolitan Museum of Art, New York*

Abraham Lincoln, lest we forget, was a politician as well as a statesman. Instrumental in organizing the Republican Party in Illinois in 1856, he ran as its candidate for U.S. senator two years later. His seven campaign debates with Democrat Stephen A. Douglas over the slavery issue were a dramatic highlight of the state's early history. Modern political activity remains energetic, if less eloquent, its chief feature being the geographic split between the two major parties. State politics are dominated by Republicans as reliably as Chicago's are by Democrats. The city hasn't seen a Republican mayor since the corrupt "Big Bill" Thompson finished his third term in 1931. Since then voters have elected nothing but Democrats—mostly Daleys—to the post.

Richard J. Daley, mayor from 1955 to 1976, remains fixed in the public mind as the "boss," running the city through a system of so-called Machine politics and clout, rewarding allies with patronage jobs and delivering the vote for Democratic presidential candidates. His son, Richard M. Daley, became mayor in 1989 and has been faithfully reelected ever since. Between the Daley reigns came two important firsts: Jane Byrne, the city's first female mayor, and Harold Washington, the first African American to hold the post. 🦜

"HE DOESN'T USE THE MAIN ENTRANCE BECAUSE THE people would jump up, clutch at his hands, and over-excite themselves. He was striding through the building one day when a little man sprung past the bodyguards and kissed his hand."

Mike Royko, Boss: Richard J. Daley of Chicago, *1971*

The Passionate Reformer

Social reformer Jane Addams, who with Ellen Gates Starr opened the Hull House set-tlement on Chicago's West Side in 1889, was a passionate spokesperson for labor reform. Her work led to the opening of free employment offices, the regulation of sweatshops, inspection of factories, and other social legislation. Addams vociferously took the side of the accused Hay-market bombers—advocates of socialism, anarchism, and the eight-hour workday—who in 1886 were sentenced to death for participating in a rally at which a bomb had been thrown, resulting in 11 deaths.

Right: X Marks the Spot: Chicago Gang Wars in Pictures, pulp glorification of gangsters, c. 1930. Chicago Historical Society Below: Robert Stack as Eliot Ness in The Untouchables TV series. Photofest. Opposite above: Warren Oates et al. in the 1973 movie Dillinger. Photofest. Opposite below: Mug shots of Al Capone, 1931. Chicago Historical Society

To many people, Chicago is still Gangsterland, U.S.A., and the era of Prohibition, Al Capone, and the St. Valentine's Day Massacre seems as vivid as if it had just ended last week. It's an impression largely created and kept alive by movies, though the reality of bloody street shoot-outs and gaudy gangland funerals was theatrical enough. The epic war waged between U.S. Treasury agent Eliot Ness and Capone, who ruled a criminal empire of bootlegging, gambling, and prostitution, was riveting even before Ness chronicled his side of the story in *The Untouchables.*

With the Depression came a new kind of gangster—the bank robber, John Dillinger being the most notorious. Dillinger's demise was even more explicitly cinematic than Capone's. He was gunned down by FBI agents in the alley outside the

CHICAGO Gang Wars in Pictures

marks the Spot

Biograph Theatre on Chicago's North Side after a showing of the movie *Manhattan Melodrama*, which he had just seen with his girlfriend and her landlady. That landlady, Anna Sage, soon became known as the "lady in red" who tipped off the Feds. ♟

"*You can get further with a kind word* and a gun than you can with just a kind word."

Al Capone (Robert De Niro) in dialogue
from The Untouchables, *1987*

Who's Who in Gangsterland

Al Capone, a.k.a. "Scarface"
Chicago crime overlord

"Big Jim" Colosimo
Ran brothels, labor union scams; bagman for corrupt politicians

Jake "Greasy Thumb" Guzik
Capone's bookkeeper

Alfred "Jake" Lingle
Mob-linked Tribune reporter, shot to death by man dressed as a priest

George "Bugs" Moran
Seven members of his mob were executed by Capone henchmen in the 1929 St. Valentine's Day Massacre

Frank "The Enforcer" Nitti
Capone's successor broadened gang operations to include labor racketeering, gambling, extortion, prostitution

Dion O'Banion
Capone rival shot to death in his flower shop opposite Holy Name Cathedral

The Narret residence, designed by Strey Builders, 1927, is typical of brick bungalows built in northwestern Chicago. *Photo Matt Herman. Right:* Mies van der Rohe's design for the Farnsworth House in Plano, south of Chicago, epitomizes the architect's spare aesthetic. Made of steel, glass, and travertine, it was completed in 1951. *Photo Karen Hirsch*

The Chicago invention of "balloon frame" methods in the 1830s revolutionized construction, especially when it came to building houses. Instead of the heavy timber frames and mortise-and-tenon joints that characterized early settlers' log buildings, "Chicago construction" used thin studs held together by nails, allowing buildings to be erected very quickly by unskilled workers. The first balloon-frame structure was the 1833 St. Mary Catholic Church at State

and Lake streets in Chicago.

As the decades passed, distinctive residential characters emerged in the city and downstate. Small-town houses usually mirrored in style the residents' original homes back east and down south. In some cases, specific European roots were expressed—Swiss, in Highland; Swedish, in Bishop Hill; German, near Fairbury and Morton. In Chicago, especially after the fire of 1871, masonry construction became ubiquitous. More than in other cities, the vernacular architecture of vast swaths of Chicago consists of brick bungalows, brick two- and three-flats, and large brick apartment buildings. Examples of remarkable residential architecture abound in the city and outside it. Wilmette is home to the 1935 Herbert Bruning House, an American International Style masterpiece designed by Fred Keck. In Springfield one finds Frank Lloyd Wright's Susan Lawrence Dana House; and in Plano, Mies van der Rohe's airy 1951 Farnsworth House. 🎩

Chicago row houses. Housing styles in the city vary by neighborhood, with vintage and new high-rises crowding the lakefront; townhouses and two-flats dominating older, inland neighborhoods; and single-family brick and frame houses farther out. *Photo Bruce Mathews/Midwestock*

The Charles B. Pikes garden by David Adler, 1917, frames a view of Lake Michigan in the North Shore suburb of Lake Forest. *Chicago Historical Society. Photo Hedrich-Blessing*

Splendor in the Grass

Chicago's motto, "Urbs in Horto"—city in a garden—is a bit of a stretch. For truly glamorous greenery one looks to the North Shore suburbs and other enclaves of wealth. One verdant Lake Forest estate, designed for the Charles B. Pikes in 1917, features a garden by architect David Adler; its sweeping lawns, statuary, and close-clipped yews frame a dramatic view of the lake. Also in Lake Forest, Ragdale is an artists' retreat adjacent to 30 acres of virgin prairie. Originally the home of architect Howard Van Doren Shaw, the 1897–98 Arts-and-

Crafts-inspired buildings are surrounded by fanciful gardens and outdoor spaces. Not far away, in Vernon Hills, is the Cuneo Museum and Gardens, originally an estate built in 1914–17 for millionaire Samuel Insull. The elaborate grounds surround a Mediterranean-style mansion designed by architect Benjamin Marshall, who also did the Drake Hotel in Chicago.

Hundreds of miles away, the Georgian-style Allerton House (1900) is part of a 12,000-acre spread on the Sangamon River, near Monticello, called "The Farms." The estate was a labor of love for Robert Allerton, son of a Chicago livestock baron. Its 1,600 acres of formal gardens, prairie, and sculpture garden are open to the public.

Above: **The grounds of Cantigny, estate of longtime** *Chicago Tribune* **publisher Robert McCormick, in west suburban Wheaton. McCormick named his estate, which also houses a military museum, after a World War I battlefield.** *Photo Allen Rokach. Left:* **Exterior of Ragdale. The grounds of Ragdale, an artists' retreat, include acreage of virgin prairie and restored meadowland.** *Photo Ray F. Hillstrom, Jr.*

"An idea is salvation by imagination."

Frank Lloyd Wright, An Autobiography, 1932

The father of the Prairie School, Frank Lloyd Wright is rare among the gods of architecture in that his enormous output—nearly 500 designs built—included so many private residences. The architect of the space-age Guggenheim Museum in New York and the Johnson Wax headquarters in Racine, Wisconsin, is known in Illinois primarily for the open floor plans, horizontal lines, and asymmetry of his single-family houses, both lavish and modest. His home and studio attract thousands of visitors every year to Oak Park, where the Unity Temple and many more of his residences are located.

Born in Richland Center, Wisconsin, in 1867, Wright quit college to come to Chicago in 1887. Soon he was working as a designer for the architectural firm of Adler and Sullivan; in 1893 he left to start his own firm, also in Chicago. At the core of Wright's "organic architecture" philosophy was the belief that a building should develop out of its natural surroundings. The interior furnishings and fixtures

of his houses were as carefully conceived as their exteriors.
Two of his most notable local Prairie School residences
are the Coonley House (1908) in Riverside and the Robie
House (1909) in Chicago. ♟

"MAKE THE WALLS OF BRICK THAT THE FIRE
touched to tawny gold or ruddy tan, the
choicest of all earth's hues. They will not rise
rudely above the sod as though shot from
beneath by a catapult, but recognize the surface of the ground on which they stand."

*Frank Lloyd Wright, "The Modern Home as a Work
of Art," lecture to the Chicago Women's Club, 1902*

Above: Wright's artful rendering of the Ward W. Willits
residence in Highland Park, 1902. *Right:* Dining room of
Wright's home in Oak Park, 1889. *Photo Hedrich-Blessing
Both, courtesy the Frank Lloyd Wright Foundation, Scottsdale,
Arizona. Opposite:* Stained-glass window in the Susan
Lawrence Dana House, 1902. *Photo Doug Carr/The Dana-
Thomas House and the Illinois Historic Preservation Agency*

The Illinois Table

For the most part, Illinois is a meat-and-potatoes paradise. Downstate, barbecue rules; over near the Iowa border, deep-

fried pork tenderloin sandwiches are a standard menu item. Authentic regional dishes, when you can find them, might also include pan-fried lake perch, steamed corn on the cob, and, if you're lucky, rhubarb-custard pie.

Chicago is known for two separate strains of good eating. One is the damn-the-torpedoes cuisine best exemplified by its local specialties: deep-dish pizza, Italian beef sandwiches, all-beef hot dogs piled high with condiments and sprinkled with celery salt, and the densest, richest cheesecake you ever stuck a fork

into. The annual summer festival Taste of Chicago, which sells sample-sized portions of fare from some of the city's 6,500 restaurants, draws heavy crowds that leave feeling even heavier. But high-cholesterol treats aside, the city is serious about its food, with sophisticated restaurants in every price range presenting cuisines from all over the globe and fusions thereof. Forty years ago, "ethnic dining" in the city meant German or Italian; now it can mean anything from Malaysian to Alsatian to Tibetan and anything in between. As diners have become more demanding, chefs have risen to the challenge, offering ever more adventurous dishes to please them.

Above: **Taste of Chicago, an annual summertime event.** *Photo Tim Beiber/Image Bank* *Opposite above:* **The Berghoff,** a Loop favorite since 1898. *Courtesy Jan Berghoff. Opposite below:* **Eli's Cheesecake.** *Photo Travis Garth*

Crusty Duck Hash

Chef-owner Susan Goss of Chicago's "ethnic American" restaurant Zinfandel created this dish.

4 cups cooked, shredded duck
4 cups diced red potatoes, skin on
4 tbs. olive oil
1 tbs. chili powder
1 cup thinly sliced red onions
½ cup each thinly sliced red, yellow, and green pepper
1 tbs. minced garlic
¼ cup barbecue sauce
2 tbs. each Worcestershire sauce, chopped parsley, and basil
1 tsp. salt
½ tsp. ground black pepper
1 cup mashed potatoes

Toss red potatoes with 2 tbs. olive oil and chili powder. Roast on baking sheet till tender, about 20 minutes in 400 degree oven. Saute onions and peppers in 2 tbs. olive oil about 10 minutes; add garlic, saute 2 more minutes. Let cool. Combine onion-pepper mix, red potatoes, duck, barbecue sauce, Worcestershire sauce, parsley, basil, salt, and pepper. Add mashed potatoes; blend well. Divide mixture into 8 portions; shape into patties. Refrigerate them on baking sheet, covered, 1 hour or overnight. Saute patties in olive oil until crusty on both sides. Drain and serve hot.

An old-fashioned, mostly nonelectronic scoreboard looms over the bleacher seats at Wrigley Field, which has had lights for night baseball games only since 1988. *Photo Flip Chalfant/Image Bank Below:* Shoeless Joe Jackson of the Chicago White Sox, c. 1915, when he joined the team. *Photo Chicago Daily News. Chicago Historical Society*

"Say it ain't so, Joe."

A young fan to legendary outfielder Shoeless Joe Jackson, as he left the courthouse after confessing his involvement, along with his "Black Sox" teammates, in the 1919 World Series scandal

The Big Leagues

On any sunny summer afternoon at Wrigley Field, capacity crowds turn out to watch a team that hasn't been in a World Series since 1945, hasn't won one since 1908. What are Cubs fans there to see? Individual heroes, of course, but also major-league action on an intimate scale. With its ivy-clad brick walls and quaint, mostly nonelectronic scoreboard, Wrigley Field is indisputably charming. Over on the South Side, the White Sox have always gotten by more on grown-up grit than on charm. The team won a pennant within memory of many Chicagoans still alive (in 1959), and its dark past—the thrown 1919 World Series—is mostly a dim memory. The new, nostalgia-proof Comiskey Park has a scoreboard that explodes with fireworks when the Sox hit a home run.

The Bears football squad braves the elements at Soldier Field, as does the much newer (and lately more successful) pro soccer team, the Fire. At the flashy new United Center, the Blackhawks put cold steel to ice and the basketballing Bulls, led by graceful, high-scoring Michael Jordan, leaped and dunked to championship glory a freakish number of times during the 1990s.

Above: Walter Payton, the great running back of the Chicago Bears, gets a message from the team's mascot before a game with the St. Louis Cardinals, 1978. *Corbis-Bettmann. Left:* Statue of Michael Jordan (detail) at the United Center, Chicago. Larger than life even in life, Jordan replaced Al Capone in the world's imagination as an emblem of Chicago. *Photo Bruce Leighty/Midwestock*

"OUT IN CENTRAL ILLINOIS...AT AGE seven, I made a mad, fateful blunder. I fell ankle over elbows in love with the Cubs....I plighted my troth to a baseball team destined to dash the cup of life's joy from my lips."

George F. Will, The Pursuit of Happiness and Other Sobering Thoughts, *1974*

The famous pig races at the Illinois State Fair. *Richard Hamilton Smith/ Corbis. Below:* Ukrainian-Americans in ethnic dress celebrate a confirmation at the St. Volodymyr Ukrainian Orthodox Cathedral. Chicago's many ethnic neighborhoods host food- and music-filled street festivals that draw large crowds every summer. *Photo John Lewis Stage/Image Bank*

Fairs and Frivolities

The Illinois State Fair, held annually in Springfield, celebrates the state's rural roots with full-tilt gusto. It has everything that has made such fairs a hallowed part of America's agricultural past—livestock competitions, 4-H exhibits, hucksters selling the latest gizmo to wary spectators. But it also has pig races. Who can resist the sight of porkers chasing an Oreo?

Chicago has had its favorite diversions, too. The old Riverview amusement park on the North Side, built in 1904, promised thrills, chills, and perhaps even some actual danger. Its Pair-o-Chutes ride, fearsome Bobs, and the enormous, glowering face of Aladdin looking down over his fun-house "Castle" probably haunt many people's dreams—all that remains of the rough-edged, unsanitized, extremely popular park, which closed in 1967, replaced by a shopping mall.

Past and present meet at Navy Pier, whose conversion to its current, family-friendly use in the 1990s must be counted a success, at least by tourists. The erstwhile white elephant of a municipal pier metamorphosed into a noisy, colorful extravaganza of restaurants, shops, boat rides, and other entertainments, including the excellent Chicago Children's Museum. Its enormous, slow-moving Ferris wheel twinkles with lights at night, visible from all along the lakefront.

Above: Visitors to Riverview enjoy the Water Bug ride, 1952. In the days before theme parks, in-city amusement parks such as Riverview were popular for thrill rides, fun houses, and sometimes unsavory attractions, including freak shows and monkey races. The thrills and chills were usually harmless but occasionally life-threatening: in 1937, 72 people were injured when a roller coaster car stalled at the top of a rise and rolled backward into an oncoming car. *Chicago Historical Society. Left:* Navy Pier. The once peaceful, if underused, municipal pier has been reconceived as a year-round entertainment venue. *Photo Scott Barrow*

Tracy Lives

Chester "Chet" Gould, an artist who'd worked at most of the papers in town, had nearly lost hope of selling a feature to the *Chicago Tribune* and *New York News* syndicate when, in 1931, publisher Joseph Medill Patterson took a fancy to his strip "Plainclothes Tracy." "When I came up with the idea of Tracy, Chicago was in the throes of Prohibition gangsterism; what we needed was a cop who could stop it," Gould later explained. His home in Woodstock, Illinois, contains a small museum devoted to the jut-jawed gumshoe.

Right: Chester Gould drew this special Dick Tracy panel, depicting the hero, all his villains, and himself, for *Life* magazine in 1944. *Tribune Media Services. The Chester Gould–Dick Tracy Museum. Opposite above:* Mike Royko. *Tribune Media Services. Opposite right:* Advertising poster for the *Chicago Daily News,* 1881. *Chicago Historical Society*

Making News

Both the *Tribune* and the *Sun-Times* have lively histories, accruing from Chicago's past as a rowdy forum for aggressive journalism. Under publishers Joseph Medill and his grandson, Colonel Robert R. McCormick, the *Tribune,* founded in 1847, was a loud, archconservative voice—an identity it has tried to shake in recent years. The *Sun-Times,* created when Marshall Field IV bought

the *Times* and merged it with the Field-owned *Sun* after World War II, was positioned from the start as an alternative to its Gothic-towered neighbor, with strong local coverage in a commuter-friendly tabloid format.

Over the years, many stellar writers have worked in Chicago's newsrooms, including Carl Sandburg, Edna Ferber, and Ring Lardner. *The Front Page*, a play by reporters Charles MacArthur and Ben Hecht (later made into several movies), captured the anything-for-a-story spirit of newspapering's early days in the city. Today, the local rags are best known not for hawkish war coverage or rambunctious crime reporting but for their popular syndicated columnists, including the late Mike Royko, advice maven Ann Landers, and movie critic Roger Ebert, among others.

"DUFFY! LISTEN! I WANT YOU TO SEND A WIRE TO THE Chief of Police of La Porte, Indiana—That's right— Tell him to meet the twelve-forty out of Chicago— New York Central—and arrest Hildy Johnson and bring him back here—Wire him full description— The son of a bitch stole my watch!"

[The curtain falls.]

Walter, the high-strung newspaper editor in Ben Hecht and Charles MacArthur's play The Front Page, *1928*

THE LITERARY LIFE

A list of writers who've produced significant works while residing in Illinois would be long indeed. Even a partial accounting would include L. Frank Baum, creator of the Oz books, and Edgar Rice Burroughs, who invented Tarzan. In poetry there's Galesburg's Carl Sandburg as well as Vachel Lindsay, Edgar Lee Masters, Langston Hughes, Karl Shapiro, and Gwendolyn Brooks, Illinois's poet laureate. The works of Upton Sinclair, Nelson Algren, Edna Ferber, Theodore Dreiser, Frank Norris, Richard Wright, Studs Terkel, Leo Rosten, Philip Roth, Lorraine Hansberry, William Maxwell, and David Mamet are all colored by their time spent in the state.

Like New York in the East, Chicago has always been a magnet for writers from the heartland. In the 1910s, the "Chicago Renaissance" writers—including Dreiser, Sandburg, and Sherwood Anderson—briefly made the town a literary hotbed. Among others who have dramatized the city's life are James T. Farrell, creator of the Studs Lonigan trilogy, and novelist and Nobel laureate Saul Bellow.

"STUDS COULDN'T STAY IN ONE PLACE, AND HE kept walking up and down Indiana Avenue, wishing that the guys would come around. As he passed Young Horn Buckford and some punk he didn't know, Young Horn said hello to him. He gruffed a reply. He heard Young Horn say, as he walked on: 'You know who that is? That's STUDS LONIGAN. He's the champ fighter of the block.'

Studs laughed to himself, proud."

James T. Farrell, Young Lonigan:
A Boyhood in Chicago Streets, *1932*

The WONDERFUL WIZARD OF OZ

BY THE CREATORS OF
FATHER GOOSE
⧉HIS BOOK⧉

The Tin Woodman   The Scarecrow
FROM
THE WONDERFUL WIZARD OF OZ
The funniest child's book ever published.

Between Soft Covers

Harriet Monroe and Hugh Hefner have more in common than many couples: both founded magazines in Chicago that still dominate their fields. Monroe's *Poetry: A Magazine of Verse,* founded in 1912, champions the work of important new poets: Sandburg's "Chicago" first appeared there, as did T. S. Eliot's "The Love Song of J. Alfred Prufrock." Hefner published his first issue of *Playboy* in 1953, correctly guessing that a combination of serious stories and pictures of naked women would find an audience.

That cool chick down on Calumet
Has got herself a brand new cat,
With pretty patent-leather hair.
And he is man enough for her.

Us other guys don't think he's such
A much.
His voice is shrill.
His muscle is pitiful.

That cool chick down on Calumet,
Though, says he's really "it,"
And strokes the patent-leather hair
That makes him man enough for her.

Gwendolyn Brooks, *"Patent Leather,"*
from A Street in Bronzeville, *1945*

PLAYBOY
ENTERTAINMENT FOR MEN

Above left: Wizard of Oz poster by Will W. Denslow, 1900. Above: Cover of Playboy's first issue, 1953. Opposite above: Nelson Algren, 1968. All, Chicago Historical Society. Opposite below: James T. Farrell. Archive Photos

Stagestruck

Chicago's renown as a mecca for experimental theater is
based largely on an explosion of bold, young, off-Loop
companies that dazzled audiences in the 1970s and 80s. Raw,
energetic Steppenwolf stood out among those troupes, with
Gary Sinise, Joan Allen, Laurie Metcalf, and John Malkovich
among its best-known members. But Illinois had a lively
theatrical scene even before "Chicago-style" drama emerged.
In the early 20th century, the Woodstock Opera House was
an important summer stock theater—the young Orson
Welles once trod its boards. After World
War II, Woodstock showcased graduates
of Chicago's Goodman School of Drama,
including Paul Newman, Geraldine Page,
and Shelley Berman. Today, all types of

theater flourish in the state, from historical reenactments in downstate small towns to classic plays and edgy new ones in and around Chicago.

The Importance of Improv

When Bernard Sahlins and Paul Sills opened The Second City in 1959, their freewheeling, ensemble-oriented improvisations on topical themes were startlingly new. Sharp, satirical sketches, often developed on the spot from audience suggestions, gave unpredictability a good name. The company, which later established a branch in Toronto, helped form the comic sensibilities of many major stars, including alumni Joan Rivers, John Belushi, Harold Ramis, Shelley Long, Bill Murray, Gilda Radner, and John Candy.

Illinois has become increasingly popular as a film setting, but the state's cinematic connection goes back to the earliest days of moviemaking. Chicago's Essanay Studios, a powerhouse from 1907 to 1917, specialized in comedies and westerns. Today no major studios are headquartered in the state, but Hollywood crews frequently shoot on location there. Chicago's elevated trains and platforms, baseball stadiums, and other recognizable architectural icons have shown up in a large number of films. An international film festival takes place in the city every fall.

Above: John Belushi and Dan Aykroyd in *The Blues Brothers*, 1987. *Right:* Newspaper writers Roger Ebert and the late Gene Siskel brought movie criticism to the masses with their televised reviews, presented in a dueling-experts format. *Opposite:* A scene from the megahit TV hospital drama *E.R.*, set in Chicago. *All, Photofest*

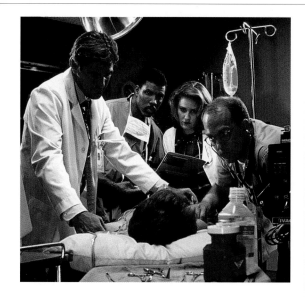

Television has also rediscovered the city as a locale, using its el platforms and skyline as backdrops for drama in *E.R.*, *Chicago Hope*, and *Early Edition*. Chicago hasn't been so much on view since TV's infancy, when its studios generated programs including Dave Garroway's *Garroway at Large*, *Ding Dong School* with Dr. Frances Horwich (a.k.a. Miss Frances), and Burr Tillstrom's *Kukla, Fran, and Ollie*. These days, the city is better known as home base for the interactive talk shows of Oprah Winfrey, Jenny Jones, and Jerry Springer. ●

Reel-Life Illinois

Movies shot in Illinois include:

About Last Night... Based on David Mamet's *Sexual Perversity in Chicago*

The Blues Brothers They're on a mission from God

Call Northside 777 Reporter uncovers truth behind a murder in this noir classic

Ferris Bueller's Day Off High-school hooky artist Matthew Broderick raises heck

The Fugitive Tommy Lee Jones chases Harrison Ford while Ford tracks down the mysterious "one-armed man"

Groundhog Day TV reporter Bill Murray tries over and over to get things right

Hoop Dreams Acclaimed documentary about real-life basketball hopefuls

Ordinary People The North Shore's sad secrets; Robert Redford's directing debut

The Relic Horror and mayhem at the Field Museum

The Untouchables Ness and Capone in pitched battle

While You Were Sleeping Pretense leads to romance for a Chicago transit worker

Musical director Daniel Barenboim conducts the Chicago Symphony Orchestra. Barenboim often performs with the orchestra as a piano soloist. *Photo Steve J. Sherman/StageImage*
Below: Ravinia, North Shore summer home of the CSO, draws picnickers and serious music fans to its outdoor concerts. *Photo Gregory Heisler/Image Bank*

Classical Strains

The Chicago Symphony Orchestra, one of the crown jewels of Illinois culture, is consistently ranked in the top five of American orchestras. Under the musical direction of con-

ductor/pianist Daniel Barenboim, the CSO draws enthusiastic audiences to concerts at the Beaux Arts–style Symphony Center (formerly Orchestra Hall) and to Ravinia, its alfresco summer quarters on the North Shore. The orchestra, founded in 1891 by Theodore Thomas, came to real prominence in 1942 under Frederick Stock, continuing its rise to excellence in later years under the batons of some of the musical world's finest conductors, including Fritz Reiner and Georg Solti.

Across town, Lyric Opera enjoys a reputation as a world-class presenter of both classical and contemporary works. Its first season, in 1954, featured the American debut of soprano Maria Callas (who said she chose Lyric because it paid better than New York's Metropolitan Opera). Under Carol Fox, Ardis Krainik, and the current general director, William Mason, the company has flourished, with tickets to its productions becoming increasingly hot; Lyric has had sold-out seasons for the past 11 years.

Above: Ardis Krainik, general director of Lyric Opera from 1981 to 1997, is widely credited with solidifying the company's reputation as an artistically superb, financially stable enterprise. *Photo Victor Skrebneski. Left:* A production of Anthony Davis's *Amistad* at Lyric Opera of Chicago (1997–98). *Courtesy Lyric Opera of Chicago*

Benny Goodman and his band playing at the Congress Hotel, 1935. *Chicago Historical Society Below:* Aragon Ballroom in Chicago's Uptown neighborhood. *Photo Susan Anderson. Opposite above: Junior Wells by* Fred Brown, 1989. *National Museum of American Art, Washington, D.C./Art Resource, New York. Opposite below: B. B. King. Tom Zuccareno/StageImage*

When Mississippi-born singer and guitarist Muddy Waters hooked up with bass player and songwriter Willie Dixon in 1954, Chicago's distinctively swaggering, electrified blues was born. Fans of the music, which has influenced rock 'n' rollers from Eric Clapton to the Rolling Stones, can't get enough of the hard-driving sound. They pack venues from the glitzy House of Blues to the unostentatious Checkerboard Lounge to hear today's blues artists carry on the tradition.

The city also has a long tradition as a center for jazz, its special sound developing out of New Orleans–style music brought north by Joe "King" Oliver, Jelly Roll Morton, and others in the 1920s. Over the decades, many of the great masters of jazz flourished in Chicago, including trumpeter Louis Armstrong, King of Swing Benny Goodman (who studied clarinet at Hull House), pianist Earl "Fatha" Hines, and vocalist-pianist Nat "King" Cole.

> Mame was singing
> At the Midnight Club.
> And the place was red
> With blues.
> She could shake her body
> Across the floor.
> For what did she have
> To lose?
>
> *Gwendolyn Brooks, from
> "Queen of the Blues," 1945*

Gospel Glory

Gospel music was created in Chicago when blues pianist Thomas A. Dorsey wrote "Take My Hand, Precious Lord" in 1932, following the death of his wife and child. His combination of sacred and secular elements—expressions of devout faith set to a syncopated blues beat—soon became hugely popular at South Side churches and far beyond.

The Open Bridge by Emil Armin, 1930. Armin was a Romanian-born painter whose expressionistic works often showed scenes of Chicago, his adopted hometown, and of Mexico and New Mexico, where he often traveled. *Illinois State Museum*

With one of the most important art museums in the world to call its own—the Art Institute of Chicago—Illinois is perhaps better known as a place to see art than to make it. Still, though few locally born painters have achieved international reputations, many significant artists have worked in the state. From Ivan Albright's densely phantasmagorical images to Emil Armin's energetic urban scenes to Archibald Motley, Jr.'s powerful

renderings of Chicago's Bronzeville neighborhood, all manner of styles have found expression over the years. In sculpture, prominent names include Chicago-born Richard Hunt, whose welded-metal works are found in museum collections all over the world, and H. C. Westermann, an idiosyncratic artist who studied at the School of the Art Institute of Chicago in the early 1950s and soon attracted influential collectors with his playfully pessimistic sculptures. Wood figured prominently in Westermann's work, perhaps due to his early years working in the lumber industry. ✇

Philosophy and Photography

The visual arts in Illinois took a giant step into the present when Hungarian-born artist and designer Laszlo Moholy-Nagy came to Chicago in 1937 to head the New Bauhaus—later renamed the Institute of Design at the Illinois Institute of Technology. Moholy-Nagy, whose own work often incorporated industrial materials and abstract geometries, saw his school as a place where poets, philosophers, artists, and scientists would collaborate, drawing on their experience of the larger world to create an improved civilization. Its

Above: Chicago 1954 by Aaron Siskind, 1957. International Museum of Photography and Film, George Eastman House, and the Aaron Siskind Foundation. Right: Midwest Landscape #60 by Art Sinsabaugh, 1961. Sinsabaugh often used a banquet camera, which produced 12-by-20-inch negatives. Indiana University Art Museum

photography department was particularly influential, with such important photographers as Arthur Siegel, Harry Callahan, and Nathan Lerner on its faculty. Other important teachers included Aaron Siskind, whose close-up abstractions of urban textural elements are considered pioneering, and Art Sinsabaugh, known for his strongly horizontal midwestern landscapes.

Right: Untitled, vintage photogram by Laszlo Moholy-Nagy, 1943. Moholy was fascinated by the interactions of light in photography and sculpture. *The Museum of Fine Arts, Houston*

Chicago's Imagists

In anticipation of a 1966 exhibit, six young artists associated with Chicago's Hyde Park Art Center—James Falconer, Art Green, Gladys Nilsson, Jim Nutt, Suellen Rocca, and Karl

Wirsum—decided to call themselves the Hairy Who. Their work was a provocatively coarse, even vulgar form of Pop Art, often showing frontal figures in jarring colors. The group, along with Ed Paschke, Roger Brown, and other artists, most of them graduates of the School of the Art Institute, came to be known as the Imagists, the

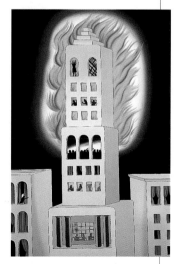

most widely recognized art movement to emerge from Chicago in this century. "To the Chicagoans the figure was no liability at all, but an expressive asset of the first order," wrote art historian Franz Schulze. "[It was] demonstrably the most nearly universal metaphor by which humans had confronted and accounted for experience since the dawn of history."

Right: Ice Skating in Winter: Clubbing the Red Sapling; Oaks by Donna Tomasello Falk, 1993. Falk's recent paintings are allegories about her experience as an Italian-American woman. *Wood Street Gallery. Below: Paintbrush Portraits* by Mr. Imagination, c. 1990s. Outsider art, the work of (in most cases) un-trained visionaries, has a strong following in Chicago, where Intuit, an organization of collectors, promotes and exhibits work by non-mainstream artists. *Carl Hammer Gallery*

For artists working today, genres, styles, and intentions overlap. As Chicago's Museum of Contemporary Art works to establish itself in austerely glamorous new digs and the Chicago Cultural Center nimbly stages an immense variety of exhibits, nonmainstream art action in the city has shifted from the fringes of downtown to outlying neighborhoods. One such area, Wicker Park/Bucktown, hosts the annual festival Around the Coyote, which showcases the work of emerging local artists. Other places to find interesting new art include Ten in One Gallery, Beret International, the Chicago Project Room, and the Mexican Fine Arts Center Museum. In Springfield, the Illinois State Museum is home to significant collections of folk art; WPA paintings, prints, and sculpture; and 20th-century works by artists and photographers with ties to the state. ❧

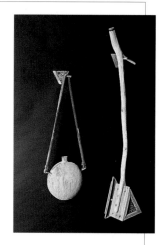

Above: Ergon, calabash and handled sieve by David Robert Nelson, 1998. *Courtesy the artist and Wood Street Gallery Left: Mary Lou* by Ben Stone, 1999. *Ten in One Gallery.* Galleries come and go in Chicago, but art endures. Many of the city's riskier show-cases have taken up residence in neighbor-hoods some distance from downtown, includ-ing Wicker Park/Buck-town on the Near Northwest Side.

Lava Lites Live On

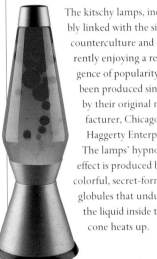

The kitschy lamps, inextricably linked with the sixties counterculture and currently enjoying a resurgence of popularity, have been produced since 1965 by their original manufacturer, Chicago's Haggerty Enterprises. The lamps' hypnotic effect is produced by colorful, secret-formula globules that undulate as the liquid inside the glass cone heats up.

Taj Mahal on the North Shore

The glistening, lacy-domed Baha'i Temple, designed by Louis Bourgeois, has been a Wilmette landmark since its 1953 completion, following decades of construction difficulties. The Baha'i faith, an independent religion, teaches that all the world's religions are, in fact, one.

Showstoppers

When a big white horse says he feels like dancing, don't try to stop him. The high-flying Lipizzan stallions of Tempel Farms in Wadsworth, which perform leaps in unison while standing on their hind legs, are the largest herd of these balletic equines in the world outside Austria; they and their riders put on exhibitions regularly.

Madam, I'm Atom

On December 2, 1942, a team led by Enrico Fermi at the University of Chicago created the first self-sustaining, controlled nuclear chain reaction. Today, Batavia's Fermi National Accelerator Lab is home to the world's highest-energy particle accelerator—and also to 60 or so buffalo that roam the grounds.

Pour It On

The world's largest catsup bottle is an empty steel water tank and tower in Collinsville, just outside St. Louis in southwestern Illinois. Built in 1949, the 170-foot tower was restored in 1995. Local resident Judy DeMoisy, the "catsup bottle lady," is a fount of information and lore about the big bottle.

Effigies in Earth

The *Effigy Tumuli* earthworks by Michael Heizer at Buffalo Rock State Park in LaSalle County are the largest artwork of their kind in the world. Giant sculptures of a turtle, snake, catfish, frog, and water strider, inspired by Native American effigy mounds, were created from strip-mining spoil in 1985.

Great People

A selective listing of mostly native Illinoisans, concentrating on the arts.

Jack Benny (1894–1974), comedian and TV show host

John Belushi (1949–1982), comedian and actor of *Saturday Night Live* fame

Ray Bradbury (b. 1920), science-fiction writer (*The Martian Chronicles, Fahrenheit 451*)

Gwendolyn Brooks (b. 1917), Illinois's poet laureate

Edgar Rice Burroughs (1875–1950), novelist, creator of *Tarzan*

Walt Disney (1901–1966), animator, movie producer

John Dos Passos (1896–1970), novelist, author of trilogy *U.S.A.*

James T. Farrell (1904–1979), author of Studs Lonigan trilogy

Harrison Ford (b. 1942), leading-man actor, best known for role in *Star Wars* trilogy

Betty Friedan (b. 1921), author of *The Feminine Mystique*

Benny Goodman (1909–1986), legendary swing clarinetist

Gene Hackman (b. 1931), actor (*The French Connection, The Conversation*)

Hugh Hefner (b. 1926), founder of *Playboy* magazine

Ernest Hemingway (1899–1961), novelist (*A Farewell to Arms, The Sun Also Rises*)

Charlton Heston (b. 1924), actor (*The Ten Commandments, Ben-Hur*)

Helen Hokinson (1900–1949), *New Yorker* cartoonist

James Jones (1921–1977), author of *From Here to Eternity*

Vachel Lindsay (1879–1931), poet ("Abraham Lincoln Walks at Midnight," "The Congo")

Archibald MacLeish (1892–1982), poet, dramatist (*J.B., Scratch*), and critic

David Mamet (b. 1947), hard-boiled playwright (*American Buffalo, Glengarry Glen Ross*)

Don Marquis (1878–1937), newspaper humorist, creator of the archy and mehitabel characters

Harriet Monroe (1860–1936), founder of *Poetry* magazine

Bill Murray (b. 1950), comedian and actor

Frank Norris (1870–1902), novelist; wrote *McTeague, The Pit*

Mike Royko (1932–1997), newspaper columnist, author (*Boss, Sez Who? Sez Me*)

Carl Sandburg (1878–1967), poet, Lincoln biographer

Sam Shepard (b. 1943), playwright (*True West*), actor

Bobby Short (b. 1924), cabaret pianist, vocalist

Lorado Taft (1860–1936), sculptor, created *Black Hawk* for Rock River site

...and Great Places

Some interesting derivations of Illinois place names.

Astoria   Named for John Jacob Astor, who founded the American Fur Company in the early 19th century.

Boone   Named for Daniel Boone, who helped lead settlers into new areas.

Bureau   This town takes its name from French trader Pierre de Beuro, who set up a trading post on the site.

Cairo   Early settlers to the southernmost tip of the state thought it resembled the landscape of Cairo, Egypt.

Cicero   Named for Roman statesman and scholar Marcus Tullius Cicero (106 B.C.–43 B.C.).

Crete   In 1843, founder Willard Irwyn Wood chose a name for the town by opening his New Testament at random and pointing—to Acts 27, which mentions the Greek island of Crete.

Cuba   In its earliest days the region was surrounded by ponds, like an island. The town of Havana is 20 miles away.

Half Day   The English equivalent of Aptakisic, a Potawatomi chief whose name meant "center of the sky" or "sun at meridian."

Joliet   Originally named Juliet, for the daughter of the town's founder. In 1845 the name was changed to honor explorer Louis Jolliet.

Monee   The name probably comes from the Indian pronunciation of "Marie," in this case Marie Lefevre, Indian wife of French trader Joseph Bailly.

Normal   Originally North Bloomington, the town changed its name when it became the site of the Illinois State Normal University, a school for training teachers.

Prophetstown   Named for White Cloud, or Wapesheka, a Winnebago prophet, medicine man, and adviser to Black Hawk.

Romeoville   The town was first called Romeo, as a companion to Juliet, nine miles south. When Juliet became Joliet in 1845 (see above), Romeo residents changed their town's name to Romeoville.

Sublette   Named for one of three Sublette brothers prominent in fur trading in the early 19th century.

Wilmette   From Ouilmette, for Archange Ouilmette, Potawatomi wife of a French trader.

Zion   Founded in 1901 by John Alexander Dowie, a faith-healing Australian minister, the town also has biblical names for its north–south streets.

Starved Rock State Park
In 1769, beleaguered members of the Illinois Confederation were massacred here by northern tribes avenging the murder of Ottawa chief Pontiac.

ILLINOIS BY THE SEASONS
A Perennial Calendar of Events and Festivals

Here is a selective listing of events that take place each year in the months noted; we suggest calling ahead to local chambers of commerce for dates and details.

January

Belvidere
Annual Eagle Watch

Elgin
Winterfest
Horse-drawn sleigh rides, snow sculpture contest; at Lords Park.

February

Alton
Underground Railroad Tours
Visitors retrace the steps of slaves seeking freedom in the North.

Springfield
Lincoln Symposium
Lincoln scholars gather at Old State Capitol site.

March

Chicago
St. Patrick's Day Parade

Glencoe
Spring Orchid Show and Sale
Displays of orchids at the Chicago Botanic Garden; experts speak on orchid-related topics.

Spring Valley
Master Walleye Tournament
First stop of the Masters Walleye Circuit, at Barto Landing.

Urbana
Illinois State Cheerleading Competition
The best cheerleading and pom-pom squads in the state square off.

Winfield
Maple Sugaring at Kline Creek Farm

April

Alto Pass
Blessing of the Bikes
Bikers gather to enjoy "Road Kill Stew" at Bald Knob Cross, Shawnee National Forest.

Peoria
Central Illinois Auto Show

Quincy
Big River Carvers Club Wood-carving Show and Competition
Area carvers demonstrate their skills and compete for ribbons.

May

Momence
Spring Herb Festival

Oak Park
Wright Plus Housewalk
A rare chance to see the interiors of several FLW-designed private homes.

Quincy
Dogwood Festival

Savanna
"Fly Away Home" Migratory Bird Day

Springfield
Scottish Highland Games and Celtic Festival
Bagpiping competition, Highland dance, traditional athletics.

June

Chicago
Gospel and Blues Festivals
Large, free, extremely popular outdoor concerts featuring nationally known musicians.

Libertyville
Water Ski Show and Tournament

Metropolis
Superman Celebration
The town, which has adopted Superman as a favorite son, is also home to a museum of Superman memorabilia.

July

Benton
"Taste of Freedom" Fourth of July Festival

Chicago
Taste of Chicago
Raucous outdoor festival at which local restaurants sell snack-sized samples of their fare.

Dixon
Petunia Festival

Evanston
World's Largest Garage Sale
Sellers and buyers fill a multi-story municipal parking garage in this lakefront suburb.

Freeport
Steam Threshing and Antique Show
Antique tractor pull, farmer-class horse show, exhibits of vintage farm equipment.

Lena
Le-Win Jaycees Mud Volleyball Tournament
Good, sloppy fun on 20 courts.

August

Chicago
"Viva! Chicago" Latin Music Festival

Chillicothe
Chilli Fest and Corn Boil

Lacon
Marshall County Old Settlers Celebration
Historical displays, carnival, parade, dance.

Peoria
Italian American Summer Festa

Utica
"Thunder on the River" Short Track Drag Boat Races
Inboard and outboard motor boats compete at speeds up to 200 mph.

September

Chicago
Jazz Festival
Free outdoor concerts by major jazz artists.

Ellis Grove
Fort Kaskaskia Traditional Music Festival
Bluegrass, country, Cajun, and Irish musicians and dancers.

Galena
Fall tour of historic homes
Get a closer look at the town's earliest residences.

Geneva
Fox Valley Folk Music and Storytelling Festival

Hoopeston
National Sweetcorn Festival

October

Arcola
Horse Farming Days Festival
Farming demonstrations, corn shucking, and walking plow contests at Rockome Gardens.

Cairo
Riverboat Days

Chicago
International Film Festival
Public screenings of works by filmmakers from more than 30 countries.

Princeton
Civil War Reenactment

Union
Cider Festival
Cider-making, baked goods; at McHenry County Historical Society Museum.

Volo Bog State Natural Area
Halloween Celebration
Ghost stories and other seasonal activities.

November

Bishop Hill
Julmarknad Swedish Christmas Market
Highlights influence of town's original Swedish settlers.

Chicago
ZooLights Festival
At Lincoln Park Zoo.

Prairie du Rocher
Fort de Chartres Winter Rendezvous
Historically dressed participants; flintlock, musket, rifle, and cannon contests.

December

Chicago
Ukrainian Christmas Traditions
Elaborately decorated eggs and other festive objects; at Ukrainian National Museum.

Glencoe
Chicago Botanic Garden Holiday Display

Jacksonville
Festival of Trees
Professionally decorated trees are displayed and auctioned.

Nauvoo
Christmas in Old Nauvoo
Tour restored homes decorated in 1840s holiday style.

Ullin
Christmas Bird Count

WHERE TO GO
Museums, Attractions, Gardens, and Other Arts Resources

Call for seasons and hours when open.

Museums

ADLER PLANETARIUM AND ASTRONOMY MUSEUM
1300 S. Lake Shore Dr., Chicago, 312-322-0304
Sky shows, exhibits, and a large collection of antique astronomical instruments.

ART INSTITUTE OF CHICAGO
111 S. Michigan Ave., Chicago, 312-443-3600
One of the city's true cultural treasures, and one of the great art museums of the world.

CHICAGO CHILDREN'S MUSEUM
700 E. Grand Ave., Chicago, 312-527-1000
A big, busy, colorfully interactive museum for kids on Navy Pier.

CHICAGO HISTORICAL SOCIETY
1601 N. Clark St., Chicago, 312-642-4600
Exhibits on the Fire, the bed Lincoln died on, and other fascinations from the past.

DAVID AND ALFRED SMART MUSEUM OF ART
5550 S. Greenwood Ave., Chicago, 773-702-0200
This museum houses the University of Chicago's primary art collection.

DUSABLE MUSEUM OF AFRICAN-AMERICAN HISTORY
740 E. 56th Pl., Chicago, 773-947-0600
Exhibits document aspects of the African-American experience in Chicago.

FIELD MUSEUM OF NATURAL HISTORY
1200 S. Lake Shore Drive, Chicago, 312-922-9410
Dinosaur bones, Native American artifacts, and visually rich wonders from all over the world.

ILLINOIS STATE MUSEUM
Spring & Edwards Sts., Springfield, 62706-5000, 217-782-7386
Collections are especially strong on the state's natural history and Native American heritage.

MARTIN D'ARCY GALLERY OF LOYOLA UNIVERSITY
6525 N. Sheridan Rd., Chicago, 773-508-2679
Loyola University's museum of medieval, Renaissance, and Baroque art.

MEXICAN FINE ARTS CENTER MUSEUM
1852 W. 19th St., Chicago, 312-738-1503
Regularly changing exhibitions of work by Hispanic artists.

MUSEUM OF BROADCAST COMMUNICATIONS
78 E. Washington St. (Chicago Cultural Center), Chicago, 312-629-6000
Archives and exhibits related to radio and television history.

MUSEUM OF CONTEMPORARY ART
220 E. Chicago Ave., Chicago, 312-280-2660
The city's most prominent showcase for contemporary art, in a stark new building by German architect Josef Paul Kleihues.

MUSEUM OF CONTEMPORARY PHOTOGRAPHY/COLUMBIA COLLEGE
600 S. Michigan Ave., Chicago, 312-663-5554
A small but serious museum devoted entirely to photography.

MUSEUM OF SCIENCE AND INDUSTRY
5700 S. Lake Shore Dr., Chicago, 773-684-1414
A coal mine, a silent film star's dollhouse, a German submarine, and many other kid-friendly exhibits.

NATIONAL VIETNAM VETERANS ART MUSEUM
1801 S. Indiana Ave., Chicago, 312-326-0270
This museum shows works of art inspired by the
Vietnam War.

ORIENTAL INSTITUTE
1155 E. 58th St., Chicago, 773-702-9521
An archaeological museum specializing in artifacts
from the Near East, especially Iraq, Iran, Turkey,
Syria, and Palestine.

RENAISSANCE SOCIETY
5811 S. Ellis Ave., Chicago, 773-702-8670
One of the few reliably high-level outlets for serious
avant-garde art in the city.

SHEDD AQUARIUM
1200 S. Lake Shore Dr., Chicago, 312-939-2438
The world's largest indoor aquarium; large sea mam-
mals are viewable in the lake-facing Oceanarium.

SPERTUS MUSEUM AT THE SPERTUS INSTITUTE
OF JEWISH STUDIES
618 S. Michigan Ave., Chicago, 312-322-1747
A large collection of religious and decorative objects
related to Jewish culture through the centuries.

TERRA MUSEUM OF AMERICAN ART
664 N. Michigan Ave., Chicago, 312-664-3939
The late Daniel Terra's collection of American paintings provided the core of this museum's holdings.

Attractions

BROOKFIELD ZOO
8400 W. 31st St., Brookfield, 708-485-0263
Large suburban zoo is home to more than 2,000
animals in naturalistic habitats.

CAHOKIA MOUNDS STATE HISTORIC SITE
*Off Interstates 55-70 and 255, and Illinois 111, on
Collinsville Rd., 618-346-5160*

Remains of the only prehistoric city north of Mexico
are preserved at this archaeological site, which
includes the enormous Monks Mound.

CHICAGO ARCHITECTURE FOUNDATION
224 S. Michigan Ave., Chicago, 312-922-3432
Information, shop, and starting-off point for architectural tours.

CHICAGO CULTURAL CENTER
78 E. Washington St., Chicago, 312-744-6630
Formerly the Tiffany-domed, mosaic-encrusted main
branch of the Chicago Public Library; now the site of
concerts, art exhibits, and other cultural events.

DICKSON MOUNDS
10956 N. Dickson Mounds Rd., Lewistown, 309-547-3721
Archaeological museum on site of Native American
burial mounds.

HAROLD WASHINGTON LIBRARY CENTER
400 S. State St., Chicago, 773-542-7279
The main headquarters of the Chicago Public Library.

ILLINOIS ART GALLERY
*James R. Thompson Center
100 W. Randolph St., Suite 2-100, Chicago,
312-814-5322*
Showcases work by Illinois artists and artisans.

LINCOLN PARK ZOO
2200 N. Cannon Dr., Chicago, 312-742-2000
Flamingos, farm animals, big game and small reside
at the city's lakefront zoo.

LINCOLN SITES, NEW SALEM VILLAGE
*Springfield Convention & Visitors Bureau
109 N. 7th St., Springfield, 800-545-7300 or
217-789-2360*
Lincoln's home, law office, tomb, and other sites.

NAVY PIER

600 E. Grand Ave., Chicago, 312-595-7437

The pier, built in 1916, is now a colorful complex of shops, restaurants, and other entertainments.

NEWBERRY LIBRARY

60 W. Walton St., Chicago, 312-943-9090

Houses manuscripts, maps, and other materials of interest to researchers, especially about the Renaissance, Native Americans, and the American West.

Homes and Gardens

CUNEO MUSEUM AND GARDENS

1350 N. Milwaukee Ave., Vernon Hills, 847-362-3054

Lavish grounds surround a Mediterranean-style mansion, Illinois's answer to Hearst's San Simeon.

FABAYAN VILLA MUSEUM

1511 S. Batavia Rd., Geneva, 630-232-4811

Col. George Fabayan's estate, originally 300 acres, once included a menagerie; it still has a Dutch windmill and an eccentric collection of antique furnishings.

FRANK LLOYD WRIGHT HOME AND STUDIO

951 Chicago Ave., Oak Park, 708-848-1976

Wright's 1889 home, designed when he was 22, contains a light-flooded drafting room and barrel-vaulted playroom; a National Historic Landmark.

JANE ADDAMS HULL HOUSE MUSEUM

800 S. Halsted St., Chicago, 312-413-5353

The 1856 house, now dwarfed (and surrounded) by the University of Illinois, was the site of Jane Addams and Ellen Gates Starr's original Hull House settlement.

THE MORTON ARBORETUM

Route 53, Lisle, 630-719-2400

Established in 1922 by Morton Salt Company founder Jay Morton, this former estate is a 1,700-acre oasis of flowers, shrubs, and more than 3,000 tree species.

PRAIRIE AVENUE HISTORIC DISTRICT

Prairie Avenue between 18th and Cullerton Sts., Chicago, 312-922-3432

Includes H. H. Richardson's 1886 Glessner House and other remnants of what was once Chicago's poshest neighborhood.

RAGDALE

1260 N. Green Bay Road, Lake Forest, 847-234-1063

This retreat, situated on 30 acres of virgin prairie, provides living and working space for writers, visual artists, and composers.

ROBERT R. MCCORMICK MUSEUM AT CANTIGNY

1 S. 151 Winfield Rd., Wheaton, 630-668-5161

A 500-acre estate; mansion built in 1896 for Tribune publisher Joseph Medill, enlarged by grandson Robert R. McCormick.

ROBIE HOUSE

5757 S. Woodlawn Ave., Chicago, 773-834-1361

One of the finest expressions of Frank Lloyd Wright's Prairie style of architecture.

Other Resources

CHICAGO CONVENTION AND TOURISM BUREAU

2301 S. Lake Shore Drive, McCormick Place on the Lake, Chicago, 312-567-8500

ILLINOIS BUREAU OF TOURISM

100 West Randolph, Suite 3-400, State of Illinois Center, Chicago 60601, 800-223-0121 or 312-814-4735; www.enjoyillinois.com; www.state.il.us/tourism

OAK PARK VISITORS BUREAU

158 Forest Ave., Oak Park, 708-848-1500

Architecture buffs head here for a detailed map of the 25 Frank Lloyd Wright buildings in Oak Park and other distinguished area homes, walking tour info, and tickets for the Wright Home and Studio Tour.

CREDITS

The authors have made every effort to reach copyright holders of text and owners of illustrations, and wish to thank those individuals and institutions that permitted the reprinting of text or the reproduction of works in their collections. Credits not listed in the captions are provided below. References are to page numbers; the designations a, b, and c indicate position of illustrations on pages.

Text

Gwendolyn Brooks: "Patent Leather" and lines from "Queen of the Blues." Both, from *A Street in Bronzeville* by Gwendolyn Brooks. Copyright © 1945 by Gwendolyn Brooks.

The Estate of Nelson Algren: *Chicago: City on the Make* by Nelson Algren. Copyright © 1951 by Nelson Algren, 1983 by the Estate of Nelson Algren.

Jonathan Gold: Recipe for "Chicago Dawgs," adapted from "The Absolute Best Restaurants in Chicago" in *Travel & Leisure*, March 1999. Copyright © 1999 by Jonathan Gold.

Illinois Writer's Guild: Excerpt from "Illinois." Words by C. H. Chamberlain, music by Archibald Johnston, 1869. From *Frontier Songs of Illinois*, collected by Joe Nobiling. Copyright © 1989 by Joe Nobiling. Used with permission.

Penguin Putnam, Inc.: *Boss: Richard J. Daley of Chicago* by Mike Royko. Copyright © 1971 by Mike Royko. Used by permission of Dutton, a division of Penguin Putnam, Inc.

Random House, Inc.: *The Jungle* by Upton Sinclair. Copyright © 1906 by Upton Sinclair. Used by permission of Bantam Books, a division of Random House, Inc.

Samuel French, Inc: *The Front Page: A Play in Three Acts* by Ben Hecht and Charles MacArthur. Copyright © 1928, 1955 by Ben Hecht and Charles MacArthur.

The Vanguard Press: *Studs Lonigan* by James T. Farrell. Copyright © 1932, 1933, 1934 by The Vanguard Press. Renewed © 1960, 1962, 1963 by James T. Farrell.

The Washington Post Writers Group: *The Pursuit of Happiness and Other Sobering Thoughts* by George F. Will. Copyright © 1974 by the Washington Post Writers Group.

Lloyd Wendt and Herman Kogan: Theodore Dreiser quote from *Give the Lady What She Wants!* by Lloyd Wendt and Herman Kogan. Copyright © 1952 by Rand McNally.

Illustrations

JAMES D. BUTLER: **19** *Landscape in Early Fall, 1988.* Oil on linen. 5 x 8½"; CARL HAMMER GALLERY: **84b** *Paintbrush Portraits* by Mr. Imagination, c. 1990s. Mixed media. 7" h.; THE CATSUP BOTTLE PRESERVATION GROUP AND INTERNATIONAL FAN CLUB: **87b**; CENTER FOR AMERICAN ARCHAEOLOGY: **25b** Hopewell bowl. Pottery. 2¼ x 2½"; CHICAGO HISTORICAL SOCIETY: **14** Lincoln Logs, c. 1955. Wood. Container: 13½ x 4". Gift of Don Miller; **25a** *Portrait of Black Hawk.* Oil on canvas. 36 x 30"; **26b** *Portrait of Jean Baptiste Point Du Sable,* n.d. Engraving; **27** *Indian Treaty of Greenville.* Oil on canvas. 22 x 27"; **30a** Lincoln with son Tad; **30b** *The Railsplitter.* Oil on canvas. 108 x 78". Gift of Maibelle Heikes Justice; **34** *Driving Hogs to the Chicago Market;* **36** Working model of Pullman berth. Gift of the Pullman Company; **37a** Chicago & Eastern Illinois Railroad, c. 1944; **40** *Carson Pirie Scott Store* by Albert Fleury, 1903. Watercolor and pencil on paper. 36 x 22"; **41a** John Hancock Center; **42** *The Rush for Life Over the Randolph Street Bridge;* **43** *Mrs. Catherine O'Leary Milking Daisy.* Oil on canvas. 37 x 30". Gift of the office of the Mayor of Chicago; **44** Proposed plaza on Michigan Avenue. Pencil, watercolor, and tempera on illustration board. 32 x 73". Gift of Dr. William Spencer; **47a** Ferris Wheel poster. After a painting by Charles Graham, for Winters Art Lithograph Co.; **50** Abbie Hoffman; **51a** *Portrait of Jane Addams.* Oil on canvas mounted on panel. 17 x 15". Gift of the Hull House Association through Robert G. Biesel; **52a** *X Marks the Spot* by Spot Publishing Company, c. 1930; **53b** Mug shots of Al Capone. Gift of the Field Foundation; **56** The Charles B. Pikes garden; **62b** Shoeless Joe Jackson; **65a** Water Bug ride at Riverview; **67b** *Chicago Daily News* poster by Carqueville Litho. Co., 1881; **68a** Nelson Algren, 1968; **69a** *Wizard of Oz* poster. Colored lithograph. 29 x 38½"; **69b** *Playboy* cover; **76a** Benny Goodman and his band, 1935. Photo *Downbeat* magazine; **86b** Lava Lites by Lava-Simplex Corporation, c. 1970. Plastic, oils, wax, and metal. 16½" h. Gift of Mrs. Wendall Batman; **87a** *Birth of the Atomic Age* by Gary Sheahan, 1957. Oil on masonite. 18½ x 35½"; CHRISTIE'S IMAGES: **47** *World's Columbian Exposition, Chicago, 1893.* Gouache on board. 13½ x 21"; THE DANA-THOMAS HOUSE AND THE ILLINOIS HISTORIC PRESERVATION AGENCY: **58** Stained-glass window; SUSAN DAY: **89** Starved Rock State Park; DEERE & COMPANY: **5** Cover of a promotional calendar; **32b** Deere & Company trademark; DU SABLE MUSEUM OF AFRICAN AMERICAN HISTORY: **79a** *Extra Paper (State Street Scene)* by Archibald Motley, Jr., 1946. Watercolor on paper. 17¾ x 24"; THE FRANK LLOYD WRIGHT FOUNDATION: **59a** *Ward W. Willits Residence.* Watercolor on paper. 8½ x 32". Copyright © the Frank Lloyd Wright Foundation, Scottsdale, Ariz.; **59b**; GOODMAN THEATRE: **70b**; ILLINOIS HISTORICAL ART PROJECT: **9** *The Art Class, Grand Detour.* Oil on canvas. 17 x 20"; **21b** *Summer Evening.* Oil on canvas. 40 x 50"; **22a** *Goose Island, Chicago.* Oil on board. 18 x 24"; ILLINOIS QUILT RESEARCH PROJECT, EARLY AMERICAN MUSEUM, MAHOMET: **2** *Henry County Historical Quilt* by Dorothy Kirley, finished by the Henry County Genealogical Society, 1988. Cotton, hand-appliquéd and hand-quilted. 104 x 86"; ILLINOIS STATE MUSEUM: **24b** Frog effigy pipe. Bauxite. 5 x 6¼ x 4"; **29b** *General Grant.* Polychromed wood. 31 x 8 x 21"; **32a** *N. C. Thompson's Reaper Works.* Oil on canvas. 18¼ x 24"; **78a** *The Open Bridge* by Emil Armin, 1930. Oil on canvas. 22 x 27". Gift in memory of Irma Thormann Morgenthau; IMAGE BANK: **14a**; **15a**; **37b**; **61**; **62a**; **64b**; **74b**; **86b** Baha'i Temple. Photo Joe Azzana; INDIANA UNIVERSITY ART MUSEUM: **81b** *Midwest Landscape #60.* Gelatin silver print. 4½ x 19¼". Art Sinsabaugh Archive; INTERNATIONAL MUSEUM OF PHOTOGRAPHY AND FILM, GEORGE EASTMAN HOUSE, AND THE AARON SISKIND FOUNDATION: **80** *Chicago 1954* by Aaron Siskind, 1957; COLLECTION GEORGE M. IRWIN: **33** *Illinois Farmscape #18.* Oil and acrylic on canvas. 15 x 18½"; JEAN ALBANO GALLERY: **82a** *Salad Corse* [sic] by Gladys Nilsson, 1995. Watercolor and gouache. 15¼ x 22¾"; LENNON, WEINBERG, INC., NEW YORK: **79b** *Burning House* by H. C. Westermann, 1958. Pine, brass, tin, glass, and enamel. 43 x 16 x 12". Licensed by VAGA, New York, NY; LYRIC OPERA OF CHICAGO: **75b**; MAYA POLSKY GALLERY: **82b** *Musica Rouge* by Ed Paschke, 1998. Oil on linen. 50 x 78"; THE METROPOLITAN MUSEUM OF ART, NEW YORK: **51** *Michigan Boulevard with Mayor Daley* by Red Grooms, 1969. Watercolor and collage on paper. 40½ x 40½". Purchase, Friends of the Department Gifts and matching funds from The National Endowment for the Arts, 1978 (1978.181). Photograph © 1996 The Metropolitan Museum of Art; MICHAEL MCCOY COLLECTION: **28** *Galena Harbor,* 1852. Oil on canvas. 30 x 38"; WENDELL MINOR: **1** *Red-winged Blackbird* from *Heartland,* 1989. Acrylic on masonite panel. 10 x 22"; THE MORTON ARBORETUM, LISLE: **13b** *White Oak.* Pen and ink on paper. 18 x 24"; THE MUSEUM OF FINE ARTS, HOUSTON:

81a *Untitled* by Laszlo Moholy-Nagy, 1943. Vintage gelatin photogram. 10 x 8". Museum purchase with funds provided by the S. I. Morris Photography fund. Photo courtesy Allen Mewbourn; NATIONAL GEOGRAPHIC SOCIETY IMAGE COLLECTION: **12a** Illinois flag. Illustration by Marilyn Dye Smith; **12b** Cardinal and violet. Illustration by Robert E. Hynes; NATIONAL MUSEUM OF AMERICAN ART/ART RESOURCE: **77a** *Junior Wells* by Fred Brown, 1989. Oil on linen. 36 x 30"; **83b** *World's Tallest Disaster* by Roger Brown, 1972. Oil and magma on fabric. 72 x 48"; DAVID ROBERT NELSON and WOOD STREET GALLERY: **85a** *Ergon,* calabash and handled sieve, 1998. Copper, wood, and leather. 49 x 25 x 9"; PHOTOGRAPHERS/ ASPEN: **49a**; **87c** *Effigy Tumuli.* Photo Phil Schermeister; ROOT RESOURCES: **12c** Fluorite. Photo Louise K. Broman; **13a**; SEARS, ROEBUCK AND CO. ARCHIVES: **38** Sears catalog home, 1918; THE SECOND CITY: **71a**; VICTOR SKREBNESKI: **75a**; STATE HISTORICAL LIBRARY OF ILLINOIS: **31** *Lincoln-Douglas Debate.* Oil on canvas. 60 x 120". Photo The Bridgeman Art Library International, Ltd.; STEPPENWOLF THEATRE COMPANY: **70a**; TEMPEL FARMS: **86c** Lipizzan stallion; TEN IN ONE GALLERY: **85b** *Mary Lou* by Ben Stone, 1999. Enamel on Hydrocal. 30 x 28 x 9"; TONY STONE IMAGES: **45b**; **48a**; **49b**; TRIBUNE MEDIA SERVICES: **67a**; TRIBUNE MEDIA SERVICES/THE CHESTER GOULD–DICK TRACY MUSEUM: **66** Dick Tracy cartoon; WILD PERCEPTIONS: **22b**; **23**; **24a** Petroglyph; WM. WRIGLEY, JR. COMPANY: **39b** Ad for Doublemint; KARL WIRSUM: **83a** *Screamin' J. Hawkins,* 1968. Acrylic on canvas. 48 x 36". Photo The Art Institute of Chicago, Mr. and Mrs. Frank G. Logan Prize Fund; WOOD STREET GALLERY: **84a** *Ice Skating in Winter: Clubbing the Red Sapling; Oaks* by Donna Tomasello Falk, 1993. Pastel on paper. 30 x 40"; MARK G. WOODS: **10** *Clinton in Winter*

Acknowledgments

Walking Stick Press wishes to thank our project staff: Miriam Lewis, Thérèse Martin, Laurie Donaldson, Inga Lewin, Tena Scalph, Kristi Hein, and Mark Woodworth.

For other assistance with *Illinois,* we are especially grateful to: Lindsay Kefauver, Jan Hughes, Terry Tatum, Joel Dryer of the Illinois Historical Art Project, Annie Morse, Susan Anderson, Nicole Finzer of the Chicago Historical Society, Kent Smith and Gary Andrashko of Illinois State Museum, George Zombakis of the Museum of Fine Arts, Houston, Matt Herman, and Ray Hillstrom.